TUNE IN

Learning English Through Listening

3 Student Book

Richards

OXFORD
UNIVERSITY

OXFORD
UNIVERSITY PRESS

198 Madison Avenue
New York, NY 10016 USA

Great Clarendon Street, Oxford OX2 6DP UK

Oxford University Press is a department of the University of Oxford.
It furthers the University's objective of excellence in research, scholarship,
and education by publishing worldwide in

Oxford   New York

Auckland   Cape Town   Dar es Salaam   Hong Kong   Karachi
Kuala Lumpur   Madrid   Melbourne   Mexico City   Nairobi
New Delhi   Shanghai   Taipei   Toronto

With offices in

Argentina   Austria   Brazil   Chile   Czech Republic   France   Greece
Guatemala   Hungary   Italy   Japan   Poland   Portugal   Singapore
South Korea   Switzerland   Thailand   Turkey   Ukraine   Vietnam

OXFORD and OXFORD ENGLISH are registered trademarks of
Oxford University Press

© Oxford University Press 2007

Database right Oxford University Press (maker)

Library of Congress Cataloging-in-Publication Data

Richards, Jack C.
    Tune In—learning English through listening: Student book / Jack C. Richards
& Kerry O'Sullivan.
       p. cm.
    Includes indexes.
    ISBN: 978-0-19-447117-6 (student book 3)
    ISBN: 978-0-19-447116-9 (student book 3 with CD)
    1. English language—Textbooks for foreign speakers. 2. Listening—Problems,
exercises, etc. I. Title: Learining English through listening. II. O'Sullivan, Kerry,
1952–. III. Title.
    PE1128.R469 2006
    448.3'421—dc22

                                   2006040033

Market Development Director: Chris Balderston
Senior Editor: Emma Wyman
Assistant Editor: Kate Schubert
Art Director: Maj-Britt Hagsted
Senior Designer: Mia Gomez
Art Editor: Justine Eun
Production Manager: Shanta Persaud
Production Controller: Eve Wong

Freelance Development Editor: Genevieve Kocienda

STUDENT BOOK ISBN: 978 0 19 447117 6
PACK ISBN: 978 0 19 447116 9

Printed in China

Printing (last digit) 10   9   8   7   6

This book is printed on paper from certified and well-managed sources.

Acknowledgments:

Illustrations by: Harry Briggs: 31, 35, 43, 59, 67. 70; Adrian Barclay/Beehive
Illustration: 69, 82; Tony Forbes/Sylvie Poggio: 3, 16, 34, 65, 74; Guy Holt: 4,
20; Kevin Hopgood: 24, 45, 52, 62, 81; Katie Mac/NB Illustration: 21, 28, 37,
91; Karen Minot: 11, 14, 23, 29, 30, 31, 37, 58, 77, 85; Geo Parkin/American
Artists Rep: 5, 19, 29, 59, 64; Craig Phillips/Shannon Associates: 13, 22, 40, 55;
Lisa Smith/Sylvie Poggio: 10, 41; Glenn Urieta: 7, 12, 18, 32, 49, 73, 79; Bill
Waitzman: 17, 76.

*We would like to thank the following for their permission to reproduce the photographs
on the cover and in the introduction:* Getty: Daniel Allen, (listening to music);
Punchstock: (raising hand in class); Punchstock: (whispering); Punchstock:
(group of friends jumping); Punchstock: (talking on a cell phone); Punchstock:
(holding a CD); Punchstock: (student smiling).

We would like to thank the following for their permission to reproduce photographs:
Alamy: Imageshop, 83 (mountains); Jon Arnold Images, 42 (dragon boat
race), 53 (bullet train); Ulana Switucha, 42 (snow festival); Wiz Data, inc., 42
(Korean children); David Young-Wolff, 39; CORBIS: 71 (Russell Simmons); K.
& H. Benser/zefa. 8 (fire-breather); Bettmann, 80 (Amelia Earhart, Jacques
Cousteau), 86 (hippies), 88 (jumbo jet, cell phone); Chris Carroll, 74 (Caucasian
woman); Randy Faris, 57 (Asian male and Caucasian male); Najlah Feanny,
71 (Charles Wang); Li Gang/Xinhua Photo, 80 (Liwei Yang); Martyn Goddard,
51 (sign); Klaus Hackenberg/zefa, 64; Hulton-Deutsch Collection, 71 (Henry
Ford, Coco Chanel), 80 (Tensing Norgay), 86 (The Beatles); Nancy Kaszerman/
ZUMA, 80 (Jane Goodall); So-Hing Keung, 14 (Hong Kong street); Robert
Landau, 50 (traffic jam); James Marshall, 2 (mall interior); Bernd Obermann,
75; PBNJ Productions, 63; Neal Preston, 88 (Madonna); Carl & Ann Purcell, 8
(dolphin); Tom Stewart, 54; Tim Thompson, 2 (ice rink); John Van Hasselt, 71
(John Pemberton); Getty Images: AFP, 53 (plane take-off); Michael Brauner/
StockFood Creative, 27 (omelet); Daniel J. Cox/Photographer's Choice, 14
(koala); Johner Images, 46 (Golden Gate Bridge); Serge Krouglikoff/Stone,
11; Jamie MacDonald/Reportage, 9; Ryan McVay/The Image Bank, 87; NBAE,
77 (Habitat for Humanity); Karen Pearson/Imagebank, 26 (breakfast on the
go); Graeme Robertson, 51 (London taxi); Keren Su/Taxi, 46 (Great Wall); Ian
Waldie, 51 (cyclist); Phil Weymoth/Lonely Planet Images, 38 (Vietnamese New
Year); J P Williams/Stone, 50 (bus stop); Courtesy of Girls On the Run/www.
girlsontherun.org: 78; Imagestate: Charles Bowman, 46 (Stonehenge); Bruno
De Boni, 84 (African landscape); Chris McLennan, 85; Mike McQueen, 53
(Underground station); Steve Vidler, 46 (Buckingham Palace), 61 (Japanese
wedding); Inmagine: Bananastock, 23 (frisbee in park), 48 (Caucasian female),
57 (African-American male and female); Brand X Pictures, 33, 60, 86 (record
player), 89 (moving, graduation); Goodshoot, 46 (Pisa); Ingram Publishing,
32; Medioimages, 20; Pixtal, 41; RubberBall, 48 (Hispanic female); Tongro, 27
(congee); Westend 61, 2 (amusement park), 48 (Caucasian male); iStockphoto:
Oleg Prikhodko, 38 (Russian birthday pie); Jupiterimages Unlimited: Ablestock,
74 (African-American teacher); Comstock, 6, 62, 89 (waving from train);
Thinkstock.com, 90; European Space Agency / Photo Researchers, Inc.: 66;
Omni-Photo Communications: Bill Bachmann, 44 (Thailand floating markets);
Jeff Greenberg, 86 (Ford Mustang); KPA, 88 (Back to the Future still); William
Lampas, 84 (lion); PictureQuest: FoodPix, 27 (fried rice); Stock Connection,
17; PhotoEdit, Inc.: Robert Brenner, 38 (Korean birthday); Sergio Piumatti:
88 (Hello Kitty doll); Punchstock: CORBIS, 2 (shopper), 47 (Peak Tram), 61
(Chinese wedding food); Digital Vision, 26 (breakfast at table), 83 (jungle);
image 100, 44 (Wat Pho); Image Source, 14 (couple on beach), 27 (bacon and
eggs), 48 (Asian male), 72; Photodisc, 8 (karaoke), 23 (person on scale), 38
(piñata, Denmark flag), 46 (Taipei 101), 57 (Asian male and Caucasian female),
68, 74 (Chinese woman); Pixland, 15 (hiking); Purestock, 15 (skier), 59;
Stockbyte, 65; Reuters: Mike Blake, 71 (Oprah Winfrey); David Gray, 8 (circus
performers); DANIEL JOURBET, 53 (cruise ship); Jason Reed, 42 (elephant
festival); Paulo Whitaker, 5; Robertstock.com: Ace Photo Agency, 83 (castle);
SuperStock: age fotostock, 14 (rafting), 15 (cable car), 44 (Grand Palace),
47 (Times Square), 56; Andrew Dawson, 84 (sharks); Prisma, 83 (cyclist);
Superstock, Inc., 61 (Chinese wedding); Steve Vidler, 8 (Chinese opera), 61
(Korean wedding).

*The publishers would like to thank the following people for their help in developing this
series:* Sookyung Chang, Korea; Tina Chen, Taiwan; June Chiang, Taiwan;
Robert Dilenschneider, Japan; Bill Hogue, Japan; Hirofumi Hosokawa, Japan;
Nikko Ying-ying Hsiang, Taiwan; Yu Young Kim, Korea; Ellen Scattergood,
Japan; Katherine Song, Korea; Damien Tresize, Taiwan; Nobuo Tsuda, Japan;
I-chieh Yang, Taiwan. *With special thanks to:* Mark Frank, Japan and Su-wei
Wang, Taiwan.

*The publishers would like to thank the following OUP staff for their support and
assistance:* Brett Bowie, Kaoru Ito, Kerry Nockolds, and Ted Yoshioka.

Introduction

Welcome to *Tune In!* This is a three-level listening series that teaches you the two important aspects of listening: understanding *what* people say and *how* they say it. This will help you improve your English.

Student Book

There are two lessons in each of the 15 units in the Student Book. Each lesson focuses on a different aspect of the unit topic. The lessons are organized into five sections, each one with carefully graded activities. This step-by-step approach makes learning natural English much easier.

BEFORE YOU LISTEN

This section introduces the topic of the lesson and presents key vocabulary for the listening activities.

LISTEN AND UNDERSTAND

There are two **Listen and Understand** sections in each lesson that go with recordings of people talking. The activities in these sections help you understand *what* the people say. These sections help you improve your overall listening comprehension skills.

For extra practice, you can also listen to the final **Listen and Understand** of each lesson on the Student CD.

TUNE IN

This section focuses on one feature of spoken English. This helps you understand *how* people say what they want to say. This will then help you speak English in a more natural way.

AFTER YOU LISTEN

This section gives you the chance to talk to your classmates about the lesson topic. It also lets you practice the feature of spoken English from the **Tune In** section.

Audio Program

There are various types of spoken English on the CDs—from casual conversations, telephone conversations, and voice-mail messages to travel announcements, TV interviews, and radio shows. The complete audio program for the Student Book is on the Class CDs. There is also a Student CD on the inside back cover of the Student Book for self study. The Student CD contains the final **Listen and Understand** of each lesson. The track list for the Student CD is on page 92.

Scope and Sequence

LESSON OBJECTIVES
- Identifying stores from context
- Distinguishing speakers
- Complaining politely

Lesson 1 Do you like shopping?

1 BEFORE YOU LISTEN

A. Circle the two things that sound the most interesting about one of the world's largest shopping malls. Then compare with a partner.

Welcome to West Edmonton Mall!

Over 350,000 square meters of shopping and entertainment.

More than 800 stores including: six department stores,

14 sporting goods stores, and over 30 shoe stores.

110 places to eat, a wedding chapel, and a world-class hotel.

An amusement park, an ocean-wave swimming pool,

a glow-in-the-dark miniature golf course, and an ice-skating rink.

B. Where do you like to go shopping? _____

2 LISTEN AND UNDERSTAND 🎧 CD 1 Track 02

A. People are buying things in a mall. Where are they? Listen and number where they are from 1 to 4. The first one is done for you. There is one extra store in the list.

a. computer store ____   d. shoe store ____
b. bookstore __1__   e. sporting goods store ____
c. pet store ____

B. Listen again. Are these statements true or false? Write *T* (true) or *F* (false). The first one is done for you.

1. The customer decides not to buy anything. __F__
2. The black ones are on sale. ____
3. The one on display is the last one. ____
4. The customer does not mind spending a lot of money. ____

③ LISTEN AND UNDERSTAND 🎧 CD 1 Track 03

A. People are returning things they bought at a store. Who speaks first in each conversation? Listen and check (✓) the correct column. The first one is done for you.

	Clerk	Customer
1.	☑	☐
2.	☐	☐
3.	☐	☐
4.	☐	☐

B. Listen again and (circle) the correct statement. The first one is done for you.

1. **a.** The hair dryer caught on fire.
   (b. Others have had the same problem.)

2. **a.** The store label is on the box.
   b. Four pieces are missing.

3. **a.** The customer has a receipt.
   b. The customer has had it for over 12 months.

4. **a.** There is no care label on the dress.
   b. The dress should be dry cleaned.

④ TUNE IN 🎧 CD 1 Tracks 04 & 05

A. Listen and notice how people complain politely.

> ***I think there's something wrong with*** this.
> This clock ***appears to be*** broken.
> Well, it ***seems to be*** damaged.
> This cell phone is ***a little too*** expensive.
> ***Excuse me. There's a problem with*** this rice cooker.

B. Now listen to people talking about items they have bought. Check (✓) the items that have problems.

1. shirt ___
2. TV ___
3. lamp ___
4. microwave ___
5. MP3 player ___
6. headphones ___
7. shoes ___
8. computer ___

A. Think of a problem that each of these items might have.

    1. DVD player   _____

    2. jacket   _____

    3. teapot   _____

    4. watch   _____

    5. digital camera   _____

B. Role-play. You are at a store. Work with a partner. Take turns returning the items in part A. Use this conversation but include your own information.

A: *Can I help you?*

B: *Yes, please. I bought this DVD player last week, but I think there's something wrong with it.*

A: *Really? What seems to be the problem?*

B: *Well, it won't play any of my DVDs.*

A: *Mm, I see. That is a problem. Do you have your receipt?*

B: *Yes, here it is.*

A: *Would you like to get a refund or an exchange?*

B: *I'd like to exchange it for a new one, please.*

LESSON OBJECTIVES
▸ Making inferences from key words
▸ Understanding consumer advice
▸ Giving supporting and contrasting information

Lesson 2 Are you a smart shopper?

1 BEFORE YOU LISTEN

What type of shopper are you? Check (✓) the two statements that are closest to your shopping style. Then compare your answers with a partner.

1. **The happy shopper**   I just love shopping. I always go with my friends. We wander around the stores until we find things we'd like to try on or buy. ___

2. **The careful shopper**   I give myself a budget and compare prices in different stores. I do a lot of research. I never make impulsive buys. ___

3. **The anti-social shopper**   I hate going to crowded stores and malls. I prefer to buy things from catalogs or online—and then I avoid other people! ___

4. **The lazy shopper**   I try to buy everything in one store. I hate going from store to store. ___

5. **The bargain hunter**   I make a decision based on price, and that's it. I love finding bargains. ___

6. **The collector**   I buy everything from online auctions—I buy two or three things a week. I like to buy unusual and rare things and the Internet's great for that. ___

2 LISTEN AND UNDERSTAND 🎧 CD 1 Track 06

A. Friends are talking about shopping online. Which shopping style in Before You Listen suits each friend? Listen and write the correct number.

a. Kay ___   **b.** Jeff ___   **c.** Emi ___

B. Listen again. Circle the correct answer. The first one is done for you.

1. Kay is *very happy* / *disappointed* with her shoes.
2. Kay *has done many* / *hasn't done any* online auctions before.
3. Emi *would never shop* / *has never shopped* for clothes online.
4. Jeff thinks shopping online is *always* / *sometimes* cheaper.
5. Jeff thinks Kay *shouldn't* / *should* shop online with care.

A. A consumer expert is giving advice about shopping online. ⟨Circle⟩ the advice you think you will hear. Then listen and check your answers.

1. Use your common sense.
2. Compare prices.
3. Make a quick decision.
4. Ask about shipping charges.
5. Don't worry about the return policy.
6. Choose a safe way to pay.
7. Send cash in the mail.
8. Keep records.
9. Ask the seller their date of birth.
10. Check the goods when they arrive.

B. Listen again. Are these statements true or false? Write *T* (true) or *F* (false).

1. Online purchases are always cheaper than things you get in a store. ___
2. You should always get shipping details in writing. ___
3. The safest way to pay is by cash. ___
4. There is no need to keep all your old e-mail messages. ___
5. Someone must be at home to receive large packages. ___
6. If there is a problem with the goods, contact your lawyer. ___

4 TUNE IN 🎧 CD 1 Tracks 08 & 09

A. Listen and notice how people give supporting and contrasting information.

Online auctions are better than shopping in a store.

Supporting Information

And also, *you don't need to leave home and face the crowds.*
In addition, *it's very exciting and so easy.*
Besides, *I don't think I could find these shoes in any store.*

Contrasting Information

Yeah, but *you need to be careful with those auctions.*
However, *you need to give yourself a budget.*
But I think you'll find that *a lot of stores have better deals nowadays.*

B. Now listen to other statements. Do they give supporting or contrasting information? Check (✓) the correct column.

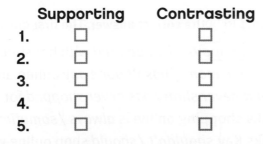

	Supporting	Contrasting
1.	☐	☐
2.	☐	☐
3.	☐	☐
4.	☐	☐
5.	☐	☐

AFTER YOU LISTEN

A. Write the advantages and disadvantages of the two types of shopping. Use the suggestions in the box and then add ideas of your own.

	Advantages	Disadvantages
Shopping at malls	_____ _____ _____ _____	_____ _____ _____ _____
Shopping online	_____ _____ _____ _____	_____ _____ _____ _____

Advantages	Disadvantages
You don't have to leave home.	You can't see the actual product.
You can get expert advice.	It's really tiring to walk around.
You can check the products in person.	Things can break easily.
You can buy things cheaply through auctions.	The stores aren't open all day.

B. Work with a partner. Take turns giving advice about buying these items. Use this conversation but include your answers in part A and other information.

a computer   a diamond ring   a rice cooker   a car   some old record albums

A: *I want to buy a computer. What should I do?*

B: *I think you should go to a department store.*

A: *Why?*

B: *Well, you can get expert advice. In addition, they have lots of sales.*

A: *Yeah, but you can get expert advice online these days.*

Entertainment

LESSON OBJECTIVES
▸ Recognizing intentions
▸ Distinguishing advantages and disadvantages
▸ Showing surprise by using echo questions

Lesson 1 That sounds like fun

1 BEFORE YOU LISTEN

Which of these forms of entertainment sound interesting to you? Check (✓) the ones you would like to do. Then compare your answers with a partner.

1. Watch acrobats perform at a circus ___
2. Sing karaoke with friends ___
3. Watch a Chinese opera outdoors ___
4. Swim with dolphins ___
5. Go to a magic show ___
6. Look at sharks at an aquarium ___
7. Watch people skateboarding in a park ___
8. Go to a film festival ___

2 LISTEN AND UNDERSTAND 🎧 CD 1 Track 10

A. Friends are talking about events. Listen and check (✓) the correct column.

	One of them	Both of them	Neither of them
1. Who is going to the baseball game?	☐	☐	☐
2. Who will enter the karaoke contest?	☐	☐	☐
3. Who is going to the concert?	☐	☐	☐
4. Who is going to the magic show?	☐	☐	☐
5. Who is going to the circus?	☐	☐	☐

B. Listen again. Circle the correct statement.

1. **a.** The park is new.
   b. They both love baseball.

2. **a.** A video must be submitted to enter the contest.
   b. The winner gets to sing on the radio.

3. **a.** The concert is inside.
   b. The group will be performing once.

4. **a.** The magician pulls rabbits out of a hat.
   b. They do not want to see card tricks.

5. **a.** The circus has clowns and animals.
   b. The circus has gymnasts and acrobats.

3 LISTEN AND UNDERSTAND 🎧 CD 1 Track 11

A. A radio host is interviewing a skateboarder. Circle the questions you think will be asked. Then listen and check your answers.

1. What is the history of skateboarding?

2. Why do some people oppose skateboarding?

3. Is skateboarding legal?

4. What is a skateboard made of?

5. What are the benefits of skateboarding?

6. How safe is skateboarding?

7. How can you learn to skateboard?

8. Who was the most famous skateboarder in the 1980s?

B. Listen again. How does the skateboarder answer these questions? Check (✓) *Yes, No,* or *Don't know* (if not enough information is given).

	Yes	No	Don't know
1. Has it been popular since the 1960s?	☐	☐	☐
2. Does everyone think skateboarding is a good activity?	☐	☐	☐
3. Is it usually legal to skate on bike paths?	☐	☐	☐
4. Does it often get kids into trouble?	☐	☐	☐
5. Is it safer than baseball?	☐	☐	☐
6. Is it a good idea to take lessons?	☐	☐	☐

4 TUNE IN 🎧 CD 1 Tracks 12 & 13

A. Listen and notice how people show surprise by using echo questions.

> **A:** *I don't like baseball.*
> **B:** *You don't like baseball? What don't you like about it?*
>
> **A:** *I think you have a good chance.*
> **B:** *A good chance? Do you really think so?*

B. Now listen to other conversations. Circle the echo question you hear.

1. **a.** Lessons?   **b.** Summer?
2. **a.** You entered a contest?   **b.** You got a great prize?
3. **a.** Dance?   **b.** Performance?
4. **a.** The mall?   **b.** A fashion show?
5. **a.** You took lots of photos?   **b.** You went swimming with sharks?

A. You are planning your weekend. Check (✓) the things you would like to do and then add two ideas of your own.

1. see your favorite music group in concert ___
2. go to a class and learn acrobatics ___
3. attend a film festival and meet celebrities ___
4. watch a reality TV show ___
5. go to an art gallery ___
6. take a boat trip down a river ___
7. _____
8. _____

B. Work with a partner. Take turns talking about your plans for the weekend. Use this conversation but include your own information. Who will have the most entertaining weekend?

A: *What would you like to do this weekend?*

B: *I'd like to go to a class and learn acrobatics.*

A: *Acrobatics? Isn't that dangerous?*

B: *It can be, but it sounds like so much fun.*

A: *Who would you take with you?*

B: *My grandmother.*

A: *Your grandmother? Why her?*

B: *She loves to try new things!*

A: *What else would you like to do?*

B: *. . .*

LESSON OBJECTIVES
▸ Making inferences from key words
▸ Understanding specific information
▸ Expressing agreement or disagreement

Lesson 2 What's on TV?

1 BEFORE YOU LISTEN

A. Check (✓) the three TV programs that sound the most interesting to you.

Sunday		Channel 5	▶▶▶
1.	**8:00**	Six people compete to survive on a desert island.	____
2.	**8:30**	Marcia runs into her old boyfriend David.	____
3.	**9:00**	A boy travels to another planet.	____
4.	**9:30**	Contestants answer questions to win a million dollars.	____
5.	**10:00**	Your favorite animated characters return for a new season.	____
6.	**10:30**	The latest in business, world, and local affairs.	____
7.	**11:00**	Amazing dogs with jobs.	____
8.	**11:30**	Is the world's climate getting hotter?	____

B. Match each program description in part A with the correct category in the list.

a. cartoon ____   **c.** documentary ____   **e.** animal show ____   **g.** reality show ____

b. movie ____   **d.** quiz show ____   **f.** soap opera ____   **h.** news show ____

2 LISTEN AND UNDERSTAND 🎧 CD 1 Track 14

A. People are talking about their favorite TV shows. Listen and number the shows they describe from 1 to 4. There are two extra shows in the list.

a. reality show ____

b. cooking show ____

c. comedy ____

d. news show ____

e. quiz show ____

f. animal show ____

B. Listen again. Answer each question with no more than two words. The first one is done for you.

1. **a.** Is the show on every day or every week?   _every week_
   b. Do they both like the host?   _____

2. **a.** How many people are there in the competition?   _____
   b. How many people are eliminated each week?   _____

3. **a.** How many kids are there in the family?   _____
   b. Does the family make funny mistakes?   _____

4. **a.** How long do the contestants have to answer the questions?   _____
   b. Are the questions very difficult?   _____

3 LISTEN AND UNDERSTAND 🎧 CD 1 Track 15

A. A TV critic is talking about how new TV shows are planned. Circle the phrases you think you will hear. Then listen and check your answers.

1. billions of dollars
2. audience reaction
3. news
4. famous actor
5. TV season

6. popularity
7. electricity prices
8. TV picture quality
9. advertise
10. successful

B. Listen again. Are these statements true or false? Write *T* (true) or *F* (false).

1. When TV companies plan new programs, they look at ratings over the last year. ___
2. TV companies copy other companies' shows and their own shows, too. ___
3. Pilot programs are shown to large audiences all over the country. ___
4. New teen comedies are likely for next season. ___
5. Self-improvement shows get low ratings. ___

4 TUNE IN 🎧 CD 1 Tracks 16 & 17

A. Listen and notice how people express agreement or disagreement.

	Agreement	Disagreement
I think it's the best show on TV.	*Absolutely.* *That's for sure.* *That's true.* *I think you're right.*	*I don't know about that.* *I don't think so.* *Do you really think so?* *I disagree completely.*

B. Now listen to other conversations. Does the second person express agreement or disagreement? Check (✓) the correct column.

	Agreement	Disagreement
1.	☐	☐
2.	☐	☐
3.	☐	☐
4.	☐	☐
5.	☐	☐
6.	☐	☐

A. What do you think determines the success of these types of shows? Check (✓) the reasons provided and add your own ideas.

Documentary

News show

Comedy

Reality show

	Documentaries	Comedies	News shows	Reality shows
1. the hosts	☐	☐	☐	☐
2. the actors	☐	☐	☐	☐
3. the story	☐	☐	☐	☐
4. the topic	☐	☐	☐	☐
5. the photography	☐	☐	☐	☐
6. the writing	☐	☐	☐	☐
7. _____	☐	☐	☐	☐
8. _____	☐	☐	☐	☐

B. Work with a partner. Take turns asking each other's opinions about different types of TV programs. Use this conversation but include your own information. How many of your answers are the same?

A: *I think the topic is the most important thing in a documentary.*
B: *Absolutely. If the topic is interesting, the documentary will be successful.*
A: *I think the actors are the most important thing in a comedy.*
B: *I don't know about that. I think the writing is important as well. If the writing is funny, the show will be funny.*

C. Work with another partner. Take turns telling each other about your favorite TV show. Give two reasons why you like it.

LESSON OBJECTIVES
▸ Making inferences from context
▸ Recognizing activities from descriptions
▸ Expressing degrees of possibility

Lesson 1 Let's go somewhere different this year!

1 BEFORE YOU LISTEN

Do these vacations sound interesting to you? Check (✓) the opinion you agree with below. Then compare with a partner.

WILD VACATION

Join an ecology group to catch wild animals and fit them with tracking collars.

Smooth Sailing

Join our air-conditioned sailboat along the coast of Malaysia. Five days of luxury.

GREEN WORLD

Be part of a group tour to Brazil to replant trees in the Amazon jungle.

WHITE ADVENTURE

Three weeks of hiking and skiing in the beautiful mountains of Switzerland.

	Sounds great!	Sounds OK	Doesn't sound fun
1. Wild Vacation	☐	☐	☐
2. Smooth Sailing	☐	☐	☐
3. Green World	☐	☐	☐
4. White Adventure	☐	☐	☐

2 LISTEN AND UNDERSTAND 🎧 CD 1 Track 18

A. People are talking about their vacation plans. Which vacation do you think they will take? Listen and number the pictures from 1 to 4.

a. ___   b. ___   c. ___

d. ___

B. Listen again. Circle the correct answer.

1. What type of vacation does Su-wei want?   a. quiet   b. exciting
2. Where is Sophie planning to stay?   a. in a hotel   b. in a tent
3. What will Li-wei do?   a. shop   b. go sightseeing
4. Who will Seth travel with?   a. a friend   b. his family

3 LISTEN AND UNDERSTAND 🎧 CD 1 Track 19

A. People are calling a travel agency to ask about vacation specials. Listen and check (✓) the topics they discuss.

1. **a.** surfing ___   **b.** accommodation ___   **c.** pay ___   **d.** malls ___
2. **a.** swimming ___ **b.** accommodation ___   **c.** lake ___   **d.** meals ___
3. **a.** shopping ___ **b.** camping gear ___   **c.** sightseeing ___ **d.** nightlife ___
4. **a.** shopping ___ **b.** transportation ___ **c.** accommodation ___ **d.** food ___

B. Listen again. Circle the activities mentioned in each conversation. More than one answer is possible.

1. **a.** feed animals   **b.** go for long walks   **c.** plant crops
2. **a.** take skiing lessons   **b.** walk in the mountains   **c.** ride in a helicopter
3. **a.** visit a resort island **b.** see interesting animals **c.** relax on a beach
4. **a.** eat in cheap restaurants **b.** stay in first class hotels **c.** take local transportation

4 TUNE IN 🎧 CD 1 Tracks 20 & 21

A. Listen and notice how people express degrees of possibility.

> A: *Where **could** you go for your vacation?*
> B: *Well, I **could** do something different this year.*
>
> A: *Do you think you **might** go to Hong Kong?*
> B: *Yes, I **might** go to Hong Kong.*
>
> A: ***Would** you go on a farm stay in New Zealand?*
> B: *I'm not sure I **would** like that.*

B. Now listen to other conversations. Will the people consider taking the trips or not? Check (✓) the correct column.

	Yes	No
1.	☐	☐
2.	☐	☐
3.	☐	☐
4.	☐	☐
5.	☐	☐
6.	☐	☐

A. Where would you go for your ideal vacation? Complete the survey for yourself.

	Me	My partner
1. Where would you go?		
2. When would you go?		
3. How would you get there?		
4. Who could you travel with?		
5. How much money would you take?		
6. How long would you stay there?		
7. What would you do there?		
8. What could you wear?		

B. Work with a partner. Take turns asking and answering questions and complete the survey for your partner. Use this conversation but include your own information. Whose vacation sounds the most unusual?

A: *Where would you go?*
B: *I'd go to western Canada.*
A: *When would you go?*
B: *I'd go in winter. I've never seen snow before.*
A: *How would you get there?*
B: *I'd fly.*
A: *Who could you travel with?*
B: . . .

LESSON OBJECTIVES
▶ Recognizing past events
▶ Understanding specific information
▶ Keeping listeners interested

Lesson 2 So how was your trip?

1 BEFORE YOU LISTEN

A. These people have just returned from vacations. Where do you think they have been? Write the name of the place under each picture. The first one is done for you.

| Mt. Everest | London | Africa | Hawaii | the Swiss Alps |

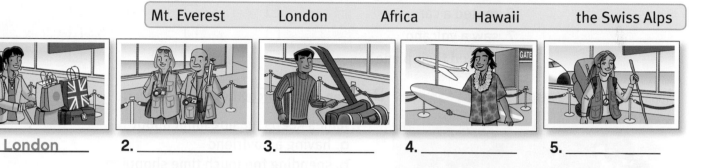

1. __London__   2. _____   3. _____   4. _____   5. _____

B. Match these experiences with the pictures in part A.

a. had some bad luck ___   **d.** saw lots of animals ___

b. spent a lot of money ___   **e.** had an active vacation ___

c. saw some beautiful fish ___

2 LISTEN AND UNDERSTAND 🎧 CD 1 Track 22

A. Naoko is talking about her vacation in Australia. Listen and check (✓) what she did in each place.

1. Brisbane
  a. went hiking ___
  b. took a boat trip ___
  c. went shopping ___

2. Gold Coast
  a. went surfing ___
  b. went waterskiing ___
  c. ate seafood ___

3. Sydney
  a. went sightseeing ___
  b. went cycling in the park ___
  c. played beach volleyball ___

4. Blue Mountains
  a. went camping ___
  b. went hiking ___
  c. spent time in an Internet cafe ___

B. Listen again. Check (✓) the correct column.

	Yes	No
1. Was she in Australia for six months?	☐	☐
2. Did she start her vacation in Sydney?	☐	☐
3. Is Brisbane located on a river?	☐	☐
4. Are there lots of beaches on the Gold Coast?	☐	☐
5. Is the water clean on the Gold Coast?	☐	☐
6. Are the Blue Mountains located east of Sydney?	☐	☐

LISTEN AND UNDERSTAND 🎧 CD 1 Track 23

A. Radio hosts are talking about their vacations. Which of these things did they do on their vacation? Listen and check (✓) the correct answer.

	Janet	James	Neither of them
1. went to Los Angeles	☐	☐	☐
2. went with a friend	☐	☐	☐
3. went shopping	☐	☐	☐
4. saw someone famous	☐	☐	☐
5. went to a beach	☐	☐	☐
6. rented a car	☐	☐	☐
7. saw a volcano	☐	☐	☐
8. missed their plane	☐	☐	☐

B. Listen again. Circle the correct answer.

1. James keeps teasing Janet about _____.
   a. having a boyfriend
   b. spending too much time shopping
   c. the songs she chooses

2. Janet does not seem to believe that James _____.
   a. went on vacation
   b. only went sightseeing
   c. met a new girlfriend

4 TUNE IN 🎧 CD 1 Tracks 24 & 25

A. Listen and notice how speakers keep listeners interested in what they are saying.

> *We were just leaving the restaurant and **guess who walked in.***
> *I was just leaving the hotel and **you'll never guess who walked in.***
> *I was on the beach one day and **guess what happened.***
> *I was on a bus and **you'll never guess what happened.***

B. Now listen to other statements. Circle the phrase you hear.

1. **a.** guess who I saw   **b.** you'll never guess who I saw
2. **a.** guess who was staying there   **b.** you'll never guess who was staying there
3. **a.** guess what happened   **b.** you'll never guess what happened
4. **a.** guess what we did   **b.** you'll never guess what we did
5. **a.** guess what I saw   **b.** you'll never guess what I saw

AFTER YOU LISTEN

A. Work with a partner. Match the beginning of each story with its correct middle and end.

Beginning of the story	Middle of the story	End of the story
1. Once I was in a restaurant during my vacation. I thought I was ordering chicken, but I couldn't speak the language very well. ___ ___	**a.** You'll never guess what he said.	**e.** Here's the T-shirt he signed.
2. Once I was at the airport ready to go on vacation, and I reached for my passport to give it to the official. But it wasn't in my pocket or my bag. ___ ___	**b.** Guess where I had left it.	**f.** So I just had to eat it.
3. Once when I was at an airport, waiting to pick up my bags, I noticed a movie star walking past. ___ ___	**c.** Guess what the waiter brought me.	**g.** So I had to fly the next day.
4. Once I was on a flight to Hawaii for my vacation when suddenly the pilot made an announcement. ___ ___	**d.** You'll never guess who the star was.	**h.** It was so terrifying.

B. Choose one of the stories in part A. What do you think is missing? Add ideas of your own to complete the story.

Story ___

_____

_____

C. Work with another pair. Take turns telling your completed stories. Which story is the funniest?

Unit 4 Health & Fitness

LESSON OBJECTIVES
- Understanding problems
- Understanding health advice
- Giving advice and making suggestions

Lesson 1 What do you suggest for a sore throat?

1 BEFORE YOU LISTEN

Match each medication with the correct instructions.

a. sleeping pills   **b.** bandage   **c.** burn lotion   **d.** antibiotics   **e.** painkillers   **f.** cough medicine

1. Take one or two pills every four hours with water as needed for temporary relief of pain. If pain continues, see a doctor. ___
2. Drink one spoonful every six hours. ___
3. A soothing dressing for minor burns. Apply to the burn area and gently rub in. ___
4. Take one pill a day until medicine is finished. Take with food. ___
5. Clean the wound and gently dry the skin. Place over the area and press lightly. Change daily. ___
6. Take one pill 30 minutes before bed. May cause drowsiness the following day. Do not drive a vehicle after taking a pill. ___

2 LISTEN AND UNDERSTAND 🎧 CD 1 Track 26

A. People are describing health problems to a doctor. Listen and number the problems from 1 to 4. There are two extra problems in the list.

a. an earache ___   **d.** a skin problem ___
b. a twisted ankle ___   **e.** a backache ___
c. a toothache ___   **f.** a sore throat ___

B. Listen again. Fix the mistakes in these sentences. The first one is done for you.

1. Take a pill ~~once~~ a day before meals. Finish all of the pills.
   three times
2. Take a pill three times a day. Use the ointment at night. Rest for a few days. _____
3. Use the drops three or four times a week. Take two pills now and then three a day with meals. _____
4. Use the lotion once a day. Take one pill three times a day. Don't drink coffee. _____

3 LISTEN AND UNDERSTAND 🎧 CD 1 Track 27

A. A doctor is discussing sleeping problems on a TV show. Circle the advice you think the doctor will give. Then listen and check your answers.

1. Avoid coffee in the evening but soda is OK.
2. Turn on the radio.
3. Take naps during the day.
4. Practice deep breathing.
5. Go to bed at different times every night.
6. Drink warm milk before you go to bed.
7. Get up if you can't sleep.
8. Take a warm bath before bedtime.
9. Sleep on your back.
10. Go for a walk.

B. Listen again. Are these statements true or false? Write *T* (true) or *F* (false).

1. All people need the same amount of sleep. ___
2. Many people need an extra hour of sleep every night. ___
3. Many soda drinks contain caffeine. ___
4. You should try deep breathing for an hour. ___
5. You should read something before bedtime. ___
6. You breathe better lying on your side. ___

4 TUNE IN 🎧 CD 1 Tracks 28 & 29

A. Listen and notice how people give advice and make suggestions.

> ***You should avoid*** drinking coffee.
> ***You should*** listen to relaxing music.
> ***It's best to avoid*** napping.
> ***It's not good to*** lie on your stomach.

B. Now listen to people giving advice. Circle the things people should do and cross out the things they should not do. The first one is done for you.

1. ~~drink ice water~~
2. stay in bed
3. use sunscreen
4. eat a lot of fruit
5. sleep with the window open
6. play tennis often

5 AFTER YOU LISTEN

A. What can you do for these problems? Write something that is good to do and something that is not good to do for each problem.

	Good	Not good
1. you have a sunburn	_____	_____
2. you have a backache	_____	_____
3. you have a sore throat	_____	_____
4. you need more energy	_____	_____
5. you have a headache	_____	_____
6. you are feeling stressed	_____	_____
7. you have indigestion	_____	_____
8. you can't concentrate	_____	_____

B. Work with a partner. Take turns asking for and giving advice. Use this conversation but include your own information. How many of your answers are the same?

A: *What should you do when you have a headache?*

B: *You should get as much sleep as possible. It's also best to avoid staring at the computer for a long time.*

C. Compare your advice with the rest of the class. Who gave the best advice? What was the most common advice? Who gave the most unusual advice?

LESSON OBJECTIVES
▸ Recognizing routines from context
▸ Identifying topics about health
▸ Expressing similarities and differences

Lesson 2 How do you keep fit?

1 BEFORE YOU LISTEN

Do you have a healthy lifestyle? Check (✓) the statements that are true for you. Add up your checks and read your score. Then compare with a partner.

Health Check ✓

1. I don't smoke. ☐
2. I don't drink a lot of coffee. ☐
3. I exercise regularly. ☐
4. I play sports at least twice a week. ☐
5. I drink plenty of water every day. ☐
6. I don't eat a lot of red meat. ☐
7. I eat my meals slowly. ☐
8. I get plenty of sleep. ☐
9. I eat lots of vegetables. ☐
10. I always find time to relax. ☐

SCORES

8–10: You're probably very healthy and fit. Try competing for the Olympics!

4–7: You're probably reasonably fit and healthy, but there is still room for improvement!

0–3: Maybe you should join a gym!

2 LISTEN AND UNDERSTAND 🎧 CD 1 Track 30

A. Commercials for City Gym are playing on the radio. Listen and circle the things each person does. More than one answer is possible.

1. a. plays sports
   b. is careful about what he eats
   c. goes to the gym every day

2. a. exercises more
   b. changed what she eats
   c. gave up coffee

3. a. changed what he eats
   b. started weightlifting
   c. plays more sports

B. Listen again. What improvements has each person noticed? Check (✓) the correct answers. More than one answer is possible.

1. a. sleeps better ___   b. eats less ___   c. is stronger ___
2. a. is stronger ___   b. has better skin ___   c. weighs less ___
3. a. girls like him more ___   b. has better concentration ___   c. sleeps better ___

A. A counselor is talking to a parents' group about ways to keep children fit and healthy. Listen and check (✓) the topics the counselor talks about.

1. number of overweight children ___
2. type of food to serve at home ___
3. health value of cheese ___
4. healthy lunches ___
5. snack foods ___
6. danger of meat ___
7. exercising as a family ___
8. best time to exercise ___
9. reasons for jogging ___
10. keeping active by gardening ___

B. Listen again. Are these statements true or false? Write *T* (true) or *F* (false).

1. One in four children is overweight in many countries. ___
2. Let children choose their own school lunch. ___
3. It is bad to have snacks. ___
4. Snacks should be used as a reward. ___
5. Let kids exercise as much as possible. ___
6. Give kids their own garden. ___

④ TUNE IN 🎧 CD 1 Tracks 32 & 33

A. Listen and notice how people express similarities and differences.

	Similarities	Differences
I get a lot of exercise.	*So do I.*	*Oh, I don't.*
	Me, too.	*You do? I never have time.*
I don't worry about my weight.	*Neither do I.*	*Oh, I do.*

B. Now listen to other conversations. Does the second person express a similarity or a difference? Check (✓) the correct column.

	Similarity	Difference
1.	☐	☐
2.	☐	☐
3.	☐	☐
4.	☐	☐
5.	☐	☐
6.	☐	☐

A. Complete the fitness survey for yourself.

	Me	My partner
1. Do you usually feel tired or energetic?	_____	_____
2. How many hours of sleep do you get a night?	_____	_____
3. How many meals do you eat each day?	_____	_____
4. How much water do you drink each day?	_____	_____
5. What's your favorite healthy food?	_____	_____
6. What's your favorite unhealthy food?	_____	_____
7. What's your favorite type of exercise?	_____	_____
8. How often do you exercise?	_____	_____
9. Why do you exercise?	_____	_____
10. Why don't you exercise?	_____	_____

B. Work with a partner. Take turns asking and answering the questions and complete the survey for your partner. Use this conversation but include your own information.

A: *Do you usually feel tired or energetic?*

B: *I usually feel energetic.*

A: *Oh, I don't. I'm always tired. How many hours of sleep do you get a night?*

B: *I get about seven hours of sleep a night.*

A: *Me, too. But I usually sleep more on the weekend. How many meals do you eat each day?*

B: *I usually eat three meals a day, but I sometimes skip breakfast.*

A: *You do? I never skip breakfast. It's my favorite meal of the day!*

Eating In & Out

LESSON OBJECTIVES
▸ Making inferences from key words
▸ Following recipes
▸ Asking for more information

Lesson 1 What do you have for breakfast?

1 BEFORE YOU LISTEN

What do people traditionally eat for breakfast around the world? Check (✓) the items that you would like to eat. Then compare with a partner.

1. There is not much difference between breakfast and other meals in Korea. A typical breakfast is rice, some soup, and spicy side dishes. ___

2. Most people in France eat fresh bread or pastries with jam or another spread. They also drink coffee with plenty of milk. ___

3. In Mexico, they often eat a tortilla (a flat corn or flour patty), beans with spicy hot peppers, and they drink coffee. ___

4. In Japan, breakfast is normally miso soup, nori (dried seaweed), pickles, and green tea. ___

5. In China, the day often begins with a bowl of warm congee (rice porridge), that contains chicken or mushrooms. ___

2 LISTEN AND UNDERSTAND 🎧 CD 1 Track 34

A. People are talking about what they normally do for meals. Which meal are they describing? Listen and check (✓) the correct meal.

	Breakfast	Lunch	Dinner
1.	☐	☐	☐
2.	☐	☐	☐
3.	☐	☐	☐
4.	☐	☐	☐
5.	☐	☐	☐

B. Listen again. Circle the correct statement.

1. **a.** He usually brings his food from home.
   b. He never eats before one o'clock.

2. **a.** He eats a big meal every day.
   b. He usually eats on the bus.

3. **a.** They eat their meal slowly.
   b. It's always a small meal.

4. **a.** She eats most of her meals alone.
   b. The meal usually lasts a couple of hours.

5. **a.** She has a large meal every day.
   b. She often has a snack later.

3 LISTEN AND UNDERSTAND 🎧 CD 1 Track 35

A. People are preparing breakfast. Listen and number the dishes they are preparing from 1 to 3. There is one extra dish in the list.

a. bacon and eggs ___

c. omelet ___

b. fried rice ___

d. congee ___

B. Listen again. What information do the speakers give about the dishes? Check (✓) the correct information. More than one answer is possible.

1.
a. ingredients ___
b. number of eggs ___
c. type of oil ___
d. cooking time ___

2.
a. ingredients ___
b. type of chicken ___
c. amount of rice ___
d. number of servings ___

3.
a. type of rice ___
b. amount of water ___
c. ingredients ___
d. amount of sauce ___

4 TUNE IN 🎧 CD 1 Tracks 36 & 37

A. Listen and notice how people ask for more information.

A: *Don't use olive oil.*	**B:** *Why not?* **B:** *Really?* **B:** *How come?* **B:** *Why is that?*

B. Now listen to people giving instructions. Does the second person understand or do they need more information? Check (✓) the correct column.

	Understands	Needs more information
1.	☐	☐
2.	☐	☐
3.	☐	☐
4.	☐	☐
5.	☐	☐

Unit 5 **Eating In & Out** 27

A. What is your idea of a perfect breakfast? Complete the survey for yourself.

	Me	My partner
1. What time would you eat?	_____	_____
2. Where would you eat?	_____	_____
3. What would you listen to?	_____	_____
4. What would you eat?	_____	_____
5. What would you drink?	_____	_____
6. Who would you invite?	_____	_____

B. Work with a partner. Take turns asking and answering the questions and complete the survey for your partner. Use this conversation but include your own information.

A: *What time would you eat your perfect breakfast?*

B: *I would eat my perfect breakfast at 11:00.*

A: *Really? Why so late?*

B: *I like to sleep in.*

A: *OK, and where would you eat your perfect breakfast?*

B: *I'd have it on a yacht.*

A: *How come?*

B: *I love the ocean.*

A: *What would you listen to?*

B: *I'd listen to classical music.*

A: *Why is that?*

B: *It's relaxing.*

A: *What would you eat?*

B: *. . .*

LESSON OBJECTIVES
▸ Identifying features of restaurants
▸ Understanding restaurant orders
▸ Using double questions

Lesson 2 Let's go eat!

1 BEFORE YOU LISTEN

Match these places to eat with the correct descriptions. Then compare your answers with a partner.

a. buffet

b. fast food restaurant

c. noodle bar

d. cafe

e. food court

1. You don't sit down to order here. Line up and say what you want. Your order comes quickly. ___

2. There is no menu here. The food is all on display for you to choose from and you serve yourself. Eat as much as you want for the same price. ___

3. Have a cup of coffee and a piece of cake or a snack. Take your time and relax. ___

4. Take a table and look through the menu. There are many different types to choose from. It's best to use chopsticks. ___

5. Walk around and decide what type of food you want. Wait for your food, then carry it on a tray to your table. ___

2 LISTEN AND UNDERSTAND 🎧 CD 1 Track 38

A. A restaurant critic is discussing local restaurants. Check (✓) which features are mentioned.

	Price	Service	Location	Food	Atmosphere
1.	☐	☐	☐	☐	☐
2.	☐	☐	☐	☐	☐
3.	☐	☐	☐	☐	☐
4.	☐	☐	☐	☐	☐

B. Listen again. What do you think the person will say next? Circle the correct answer.

1. **a.** That sounds nice. I think I'll try it.
   b. Well, I'd better find somewhere else to eat then.

2. **a.** It sounds good, but a bit too expensive.
   b. I usually eat meals at home.

3. **a.** Well, I can understand why you don't like it.
   b. Have you ever eaten there?

4. **a.** I wonder why they do that?
   b. It sounds like the sort of place I would enjoy.

3 LISTEN AND UNDERSTAND 🎧 CD 1 Track 39

A. Justin and Emma are ordering from the menu. Justin is trying to lose weight. Emma is very hungry. What do you think they will order? Write *J* for Justin and *E* for Emma. Then listen and check your answers.

Appetizers
vegetable soup ____
garlic bread ____

Main Dishes
pizza (pepperoni, mushroom,
    or double cheese) ____
pasta (with seafood, meatballs,
    or vegetables) ____
steak ____
fish (fried or grilled) ____

Side Dishes
garden salad ____
French fries ____
baked potato with sour cream ____

Desserts
ice cream (chocolate, coffee, or strawberry) ____
chocolate cake ____
fresh fruit ____

Drinks
soda, juice, water, coffee, tea (iced or hot) ____

B. Listen again. Write the correct answer.

1. How many kilos does Justin want to lose? _____
2. Is Emma on a diet? _____
3. What does Emma want for dessert? _____
4. Does Justin want dessert? _____
5. How is the service? _____

4 TUNE IN 🎧 CD 1 Tracks 40 & 41

A. Listen and notice how people use double questions to get more specific information.

Opening question	+	Focus question
What do you think of it?	+	*Would you recommend it?*
How was the restaurant?	+	*Did you like it?*
What are the prices like?	+	*Is it expensive?*

B. Now match each opening question with its focus question. Then listen and check your answers.

Opening question
1. What's the atmosphere like? ____
2. What are the waiters like? ____
3. What's the menu like? ____
4. How are the prices? ____
5. Is it easy to get there? ____

Focus question
a. Do they serve spicy food?
b. Are they too much for a student budget?
c. Are they friendly?
d. Is there a subway station nearby?
e. Do they have live music?

5 AFTER YOU LISTEN

A. Put these sentences in order to make a conversation. The first one is done for you. Then practice the conversation with a partner.

___ I'll have rice and vegetables, please.

___ Fine. And what would you like for a main dish?

_1_ Would you like an appetizer?

___ Would you like that fried or grilled?

___ I think so. What soups do you have?

___ Grilled, please.

___ Any side dishes? Would you like rice or some vegetables?

___ Sure. And would you like a dessert afterwards? Perhaps some ice cream or fruit?

___ Could I have some ice cream? And I'd like a cup of coffee with that, please.

___ We have tomato and onion.

___ I think I'll have the chicken, please.

___ I'll try the onion soup.

___ OK. Thank you. I'll place your order right away.

B. Role-play. You are at a restaurant. Take turns being a waiter and a customer, and order from the menu.

APPETIZERS

spring rolls
soy beans
hot and sour soup
crab soup
fried squid

MAIN DISHES

stir-fried noodles
vegetable tempura
curry shrimp
sesame tofu
ginger beef
grilled tuna steak

SIDE DISHES

steamed white rice
fried rice
grilled eggplant
seafood salad

DESSERTS

coconut ice cream
mango sticky rice
green tea mousse
fresh berry sorbet

DRINKS

soda
coffee
tea (black, green, or ginseng)

Unit
6 **Occupations**

LESSON OBJECTIVES
▸ Making inferences from key words
▸ Identifying follow-up responses
▸ Asking for agreement

Lesson 1 Sounds like a great job

1 BEFORE YOU LISTEN

Match the jobs with an advantage and a disadvantage. Then compare your answers with a partner.

a. cookbook recipe tester   **d.** library assistant
b. party clown   **e.** store sales clerk
c. film director   **f.** cruise ship host

Advantages	Disadvantages
1. You might earn a lot of money. ___	**1.** Sometimes you get seasick. ___
2. You get to travel a lot. ___	**2.** You might gain weight. ___
3. You can get a store discount. ___	**3.** It can be very boring. ___
4. You can make kids really happy. ___	**4.** Actors can be difficult. ___
5. You can work in a quiet place. ___	**5.** Children are hard to please. ___
6. You get to eat some delicious food. ___	**6.** People often complain about their purchases. ___

2 LISTEN AND UNDERSTAND 🎧 CD 2 Track 02

A. Women are talking about their jobs. Listen and number the pictures from 1 to 5.

a. ___   b. ___   c. ___   d. ___   e. ___

B. Listen again. Circle the correct answer.

1. Aki works from *10 P.M. to 3 A.M.* / *3 P.M. to 10 A.M.*
2. Carol's clients are *mostly young, some old* / *all old*.
3. Meena's customers complain *most of the time* / *sometimes*.
4. Danielle's clients are *all women* / *mostly women*.
5. Kim works *sometimes* / *always* in the studio.

3 LISTEN AND UNDERSTAND 🎧 CD 2 Track 03

A. Students are talking to a career advisor about the type of job they would like. Listen and check (✓) the most suitable job for them.

1. **a.** kindergarten teacher ___ **b.** circus clown ___ **c.** children's dentist ___
2. **a.** fashion model ___ **b.** hair stylist ___ **c.** aerobics instructor ___
3. **a.** park guide ___ **b.** dental technician ___ **c.** office worker ___
4. **a.** school teacher ___ **b.** newspaper reporter ___ **c.** Web site designer ___
5. **a.** flight attendant ___ **b.** language teacher ___ **c.** TV presenter ___

B. Listen again. What will the advisor say next? Circle the best answer.

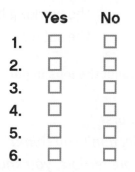

1. **a.** I'm sure you would enjoy helping people lose weight.
   b. Do you want to work with younger children or older children?
2. **a.** Why don't you take classes at a beauty school?
   b. It would be good to be able to use your sales skills.
3. **a.** Are you interested in working with animals?
   b. Would you prefer to work in a small office or a large office?
4. **a.** Did you study information technology at school?
   b. I think you should try to apply for that job.
5. **a.** What countries would you like to go to?
   b. Lots of hotels are looking for chefs these days.

4 TUNE IN 🎧 CD 2 Tracks 04 & 05

A. Listen and notice how people ask for agreement.

> *Some older people are so fit. They're really amazing,* **don't you think?**
> *It keeps me feeling young,* **you know what I mean?**
> *It makes them feel good,* **you know what I'm saying?**
> *Nowadays, there are a lot more women doing this job,* **you know?**

B. Now listen to people giving opinions. Does the person ask for agreement in each conversation? Check (✓) the correct column.

	Yes	No
1.	☐	☐
2.	☐	☐
3.	☐	☐
4.	☐	☐
5.	☐	☐
6.	☐	☐

A. Write an advantage and a disadvantage of each of these jobs. Use the suggestions in the box and add another job and your own ideas.

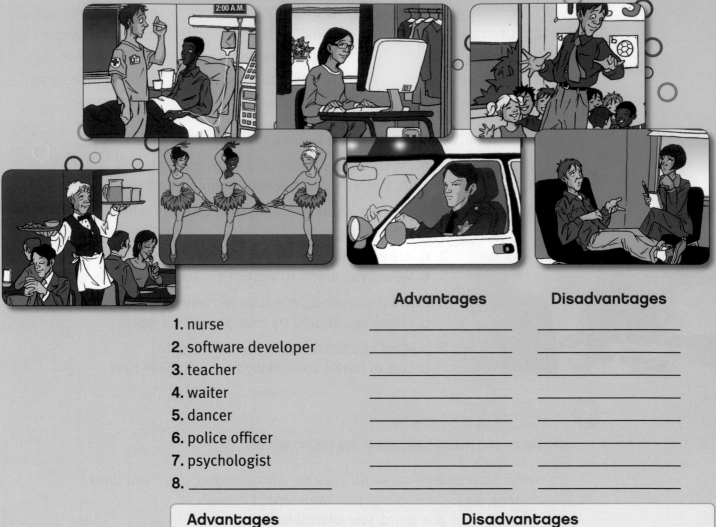

	Advantages	Disadvantages
1. nurse	_____	_____
2. software developer	_____	_____
3. teacher	_____	_____
4. waiter	_____	_____
5. dancer	_____	_____
6. police officer	_____	_____
7. psychologist	_____	_____
8. _____	_____	_____

Advantages	**Disadvantages**
There are lots of jobs available.	It can be hard to find a job.
It's really interesting.	It's rather boring.
The working conditions are very good.	The working conditions are pretty bad.
You don't need any experience.	You need a lot of work experience.
The working hours are good.	The working hours are terrible.
The salary is very good.	The salary is very poor.

B. Work with a partner. Take turns talking about the jobs in part A. Use this conversation but include your own information.

A: *What's an advantage of a job as a nurse?*

B: *Well, there are lots of jobs available, don't you think?*

A: *That's true. But the working hours are terrible, you know?*

B: *I agree.*

C. Which of the jobs in part A would you most like to have? Which would you least like to have?

LESSON OBJECTIVES
▸ Recognizing job interview advice
▸ Recognizing topics in an interview
▸ Checking understanding

Lesson 2 Can I ask you one more question?

1 BEFORE YOU LISTEN

What do you think of these questions that are often asked at job interviews in the US? Rank them from 1 (easiest) to 8 (hardest). Then compare your answers with a partner.

___ Can you tell me a little bit about yourself?

___ Why do you want to leave your present job?

___ What are your strengths and weaknesses?

___ What adjectives would you choose to describe yourself?

___ What do you know about our company?

___ Why should we hire you?

___ Why do you want this job?

___ What qualities do you have that make you suitable for this job?

2 LISTEN AND UNDERSTAND 🎧 CD 2 Track 06

A. A career advisor is giving advice about how to have a good job interview. Circle the advice you think you will hear. Then listen and check your answers.

1. Make a good first impression.
2. Bring family photographs.
3. Be well prepared for the interview.
4. Tell jokes.
5. Answer the questions well.
6. Be positive.
7. Bring a letter from your parents.
8. Ask intelligent questions.
9. Practice before the interview.
10. Wear a colorful suit.

B. Listen again. Are these statements true or false? Write *T* (true) or *F* (false).

1. Find out as much as you can about the company after the interview. ___
2. Do not ask about the salary until the end of the interview. ___
3. Ask questions about vacation at any time. ___
4. It is OK to ask about promotion policies in the company. ___

A. People are being interviewed for jobs. Check (✓) the topics mentioned in each interview.

	Interview 1	Interview 2
a. work experience	☐	☐
b. reasons for applying	☐	☐
c. future plans	☐	☐
d. job duties	☐	☐
e. education	☐	☐

B. Listen again. Fix the mistakes in the interviewers' notes.

Interview 1
a. worked in a store for two years _____
b. doesn't enjoy sales work _____
c. worked in the magazine section _____
d. studied fashion in college _____
e. hopes to become a fashion model _____

Interview 2
a. worked as a receptionist in a hotel _____
b. now works at a real estate agency _____
c. doesn't want to do the training program _____
d. speaks Italian _____
e. is looking for a less challenging job _____

4 TUNE IN 🎧 CD 2 Tracks 08 & 09

A. Listen and notice how people check understanding.

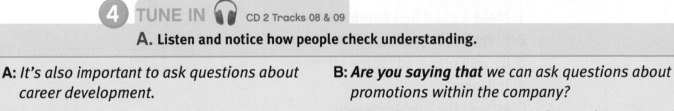

A: *It's also important to ask questions about career development.*

A: *I worked in a department store.*

A: *I'd like to take on more responsibility.*

B: ***Are you saying that** we can ask questions about promotions within the company?*

B: ***Does that mean** you enjoy sales work?*

B: ***Do you mean that** you'd like to try something more challenging?*

B. Now listen to other people check understanding. Number the questions you hear from 1 to 6.

a. Are you saying that you worked in sales before? ___
b. Are you saying you've never used one? ___
c. Does that mean you wouldn't work indoors? ___
d. Do you mean you have a part-time job? ___
e. Do you mean that you're studying it by yourself? ___
f. Does that mean you have no work experience at all? ___

A. Read the job advertisement. Then answer the interview questions with your own information.

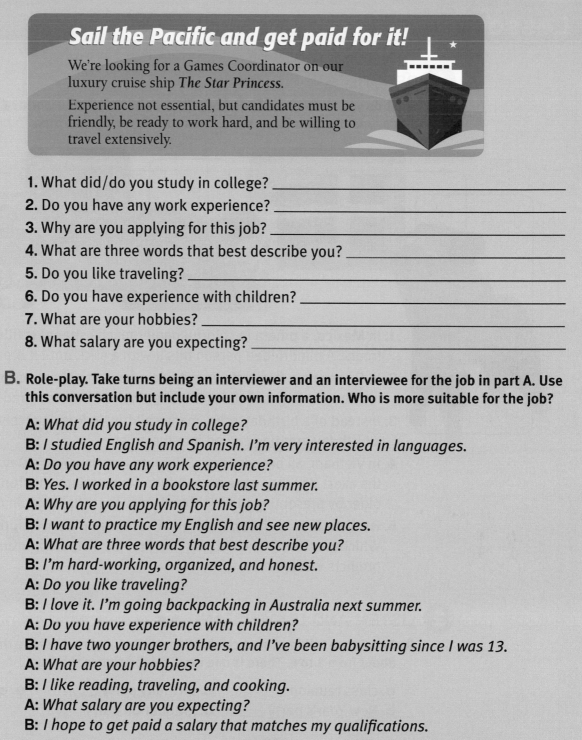

Sail the Pacific and get paid for it!

We're looking for a Games Coordinator on our luxury cruise ship *The Star Princess*.

Experience not essential, but candidates must be friendly, be ready to work hard, and be willing to travel extensively.

1. What did/do you study in college? _____

2. Do you have any work experience? _____

3. Why are you applying for this job? _____

4. What are three words that best describe you? _____

5. Do you like traveling? _____

6. Do you have experience with children? _____

7. What are your hobbies? _____

8. What salary are you expecting? _____

B. Role-play. Take turns being an interviewer and an interviewee for the job in part A. Use this conversation but include your own information. Who is more suitable for the job?

A: *What did you study in college?*
B: *I studied English and Spanish. I'm very interested in languages.*
A: *Do you have any work experience?*
B: *Yes. I worked in a bookstore last summer.*
A: *Why are you applying for this job?*
B: *I want to practice my English and see new places.*
A: *What are three words that best describe you?*
B: *I'm hard-working, organized, and honest.*
A: *Do you like traveling?*
B: *I love it. I'm going backpacking in Australia next summer.*
A: *Do you have experience with children?*
B: *I have two younger brothers, and I've been babysitting since I was 13.*
A: *What are your hobbies?*
B: *I like reading, traveling, and cooking.*
A: *What salary are you expecting?*
B: *I hope to get paid a salary that matches my qualifications.*

Special Days

LESSON OBJECTIVES
▸ Identifying types of celebrations
▸ Recognizing details about events
▸ Asking for more details

Lesson 1 It's time to celebrate!

1 BEFORE YOU LISTEN

What do you know about birthday celebrations around the world? Circle the two customs that sound the most interesting. Then compare with a partner.

1. In Mexico, a piñata (a colorful papier-mâché shape) is filled with candy and treats. A blindfolded person hits it with a stick until it breaks.

2. In Denmark, a flag is flown outside a house to show people that someone inside is having a birthday. Children wake up surrounded by gifts.

3. Instead of a birthday cake, many children in Russia receive a birthday pie with a birthday greeting carved into the crust.

4. In Vietnam, all birthdays are celebrated on New Year's Day. They don't recognize the exact day they were born. Adults congratulate children on becoming a year older by presenting them with red envelopes that contain money.

5. For their first birthday, children in Korea are placed before a range of objects. Whichever item the child picks up first predicts their future. For example, rice predicts wealth.

2 LISTEN AND UNDERSTAND 🎧 CD 2 Track 10

A. **People are talking about celebrations. Listen and number the things they are talking about from 1 to 4. There is one extra celebration in the list.**

a. class reunion ____   **c.** birthday party ____   **e.** engagement party ____
b. New Year's party ____   **d.** graduation party ____

B. **Listen again and complete the chart with the correct information.**

	Number of guests	Starting time	Location
1.	_____	_____	_____
2.	_____	_____	_____
3.	_____	_____	_____
4.	_____	_____	_____

3 LISTEN AND UNDERSTAND 🎧 CD 2 Track 11

A. People are talking about their birthdays. Who did these things? Listen and check (✓) the correct people. More than one answer is possible.

	Dylan	Lin	Remi	Ellen
1. ate some of their favorite food	☐	☐	☐	☐
2. went out with friends	☐	☐	☐	☐
3. had a party	☐	☐	☐	☐
4. saw some performers	☐	☐	☐	☐
5. played games	☐	☐	☐	☐
6. got some presents	☐	☐	☐	☐
7. got a surprise	☐	☐	☐	☐
8. listened to music and danced	☐	☐	☐	☐

B. Listen again. Circle the correct statement.

1. **a.** Jo has seen the show.
   b. Dylan got the tickets as a present.

2. **a.** Lin turned 19.
   b. The party was at his friend's house.

3. **a.** Remi knew they were planning a party.
   b. The party was at Anna's place.

4. **a.** Ellen's friends took the cake to the restaurant.
   b. Ellen got some DVDs.

4 TUNE IN 🎧 CD 2 Tracks 12 & 13

A. Listen and notice how people respond to information by asking for more details.

> **A:** *We had a great time.* **B:** *What did you do?*
> **A:** *Some friends invited me out for dinner.* **B:** *Where did you go?*
> **A:** *It was my nineteenth birthday last week.* **B:** *So, how does it feel to be 19?*

B. Now match the statements with the questions. Then listen and check your answers.

1. It's my father's birthday on Sunday. ____   a. Who is it for?
2. I'm going to a graduation party next week. ____   b. What did you get her?
3. My cousin is getting married on Friday. ____   c. How old will he be?
4. I'm going to a school reunion next month. ____   d. What type of ceremony will it be?
5. I bought my sister a gift for her birthday. ____   e. What year did you finish college?

A. When was the last time you did these things? Complete the survey for yourself. Then add a celebration of your own.

	Me	My partner
1. gave someone a birthday gift	_____	_____
2. gave someone flowers	_____	_____
3. sent someone a card	_____	_____
4. attended a birthday party	_____	_____
5. planned a surprise party	_____	_____
6. made a birthday cake	_____	_____
7. went out for a special meal	_____	_____
8. _____	_____	_____

B. Work with a partner. Take turns asking and answering questions and complete the survey for your partner. Ask for more details. Use this conversation but include your own information.

A: *When was the last time you gave someone a birthday gift?*

B: *Last month. My neighbor had her fiftieth birthday.*

A: *What did you give her?*

B: *I gave her some chocolates.*

A: *When was the last time you gave someone flowers?*

B: *In February. I gave my mother some flowers.*

A: *Why?*

B: *Because she got a new job.*

A: *When was the last time you sent someone a card?*

B: *. . .*

LESSON OBJECTIVES
▸ Recognizing features of events
▸ Identifying details about events
▸ Making generalizations

Lesson 2 What's your favorite celebration?

1 BEFORE YOU LISTEN

A. Do these celebrations sound interesting to you? Rank them from 1 (most interesting) to 5 (least interesting). Then compare your answers with a partner.

___ **April Fool's Day**   People play silly tricks on their friends to make them laugh.

___ **Carnival**   People wear masks, paint their bodies, and dance in the streets.

___ **Thanksgiving**   People eat turkey and give thanks for the harvest.

___ **Earth Day**   People clean up their town or city to promote concern for the environment.

___ **Coming-of-Age-Day**   20-year-olds wear formal dress to a ceremony and they receive gifts.

B. What are your three favorite celebrations?

1. _____   2. _____   3. _____

2 LISTEN AND UNDERSTAND 🎧 CD 2 Track 14

A. Homestay students are telling their host families about special days in Korea, Taiwan, and Japan. Check (✓) the information they give for each holiday.

	Harvest Moon Festival	Lantern Festival	Doll Festival
1. People eat special food.	☐	☐	☐
2. It helps to keep evil spirits away.	☐	☐	☐
3. There is music and lights.	☐	☐	☐
4. Part of it takes place at the beach.	☐	☐	☐
5. There is dancing.	☐	☐	☐
6. People wear traditional clothes.	☐	☐	☐

B. Listen again. Circle the correct statement.

1. **a.** The festival is only for country people.
   b. People go to family graves to honor their ancestors.

2. **a.** The festival lasts for only one day.
   b. Some of the lanterns are made by children.

3. **a.** The dolls are kept on display all year.
   b. The boats contain a lot of dolls.

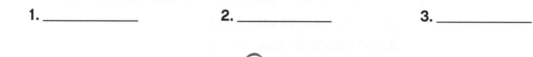

3 LISTEN AND UNDERSTAND 🎧 CD 2 Track 15

A. Visitors are asking people about different celebrations. Listen and check (✓) the information that is given about each event.

1. Children's Day

2. Snow Festival

3. Elephant Festival

4. Dragon Boat Festival

	1	2	3	4
a. location	☐	☐	☐	☐
b. clothes/costumes	☐	☐	☐	☐
c. origin	☐	☐	☐	☐
d. competition	☐	☐	☐	☐
e. time of year	☐	☐	☐	☐
f. music	☐	☐	☐	☐

B. Listen again. Are these statements true or false? Write *T* (true) or *F* (false).

1. Children make special food for their parents. ___

2. The statues are very small. ___

3. The elephants play sports. ___

4. It was started to keep evil spirits away. ___

4 TUNE IN 🎧 CD 2 Tracks 16 & 17

A. Listen and notice how people make generalizations.

> Family members **usually** come from all over the country.
> **Generally speaking,** thousands of people come to watch the festival.
> **The majority of** people eat special food.
> **As a rule,** people wear traditional clothes.

B. Now listen to other statements. Does the person make a generalization in each conversation? Check (✓) the correct column.

	Yes	No
1.	☐	☐
2.	☐	☐
3.	☐	☐
4.	☐	☐
5.	☐	☐
6.	☐	☐

A. Work with a partner. Think of a new holiday to celebrate each year. Answer the questions.

1. Who is the holiday for? _____
2. What special clothes do people wear? _____
3. Where does it take place? _____
4. When does it happen? _____
5. What type of music is played? _____
6. What type of food is eaten? _____
7. What type of competition is held? _____
8. What activities take place? _____
9. What is the holiday called? _____

B. Work with another pair. Take turns talking about your new holidays. Use this conversation but include your own information.

A: *Who is the holiday for?*
B: *As a rule, our holiday is for teenagers.*
A: *What special clothes do people wear?*
B: *The majority of people wear whatever they want.*
A: *Where does it take place?*
B: *It usually takes place in a park.*
A: *When does it happen?*
B: *. . .*

Places of Interest

LESSON OBJECTIVES
▸ Understanding tour plans
▸ Understanding a tour guide
▸ Expressing uncertainty

Lesson 1 What's worth seeing here?

1 BEFORE YOU LISTEN

A. Do these places in Bangkok sound interesting to you? Rank them from 1 (the most interesting) to 5 (the least interesting).

___ **National Museum**   Has a beautiful collection of Thailand's sculptural and decorative arts.

___ **Wat Pho**   Bangkok's biggest temple has a huge reclining Buddha statue (46 meters long).

___ **Floating markets**   Hundreds of boats float by selling souvenirs and fresh produce.

___ **Grand Palace**   It contains government offices, royal residences, and the Emerald Buddha.

___ **Vimanmek Teak Mansion**   One of the world's largest golden teak buildings.

B. What are three interesting places in the capital city of your country?

1. _____   3. _____

2. _____

2 LISTEN AND UNDERSTAND 🎧 CD 2 Track 18

A. Recorded information is being played at a tourist office. Listen and complete the information.

	Opening times	Price for children	Price for adults
1. Car Museum	_____	_____	_____
2. Science & Technology Museum	_____	_____	_____
3. Underwater World	_____	_____	_____
4. Golden Lion Movie Studio	_____	_____	_____

B. Listen again. Circle the correct answers.

1. How long does it take to get to the Car Museum?
   a. 30 minutes   **b.** an hour   **c.** 20 minutes

2. Which collection can you see at the Science & Technology Museum?
   a. cars   **b.** airplanes   **c.** houses

3. What can you *not* see at Underwater World?
   a. sharks   **b.** dolphins   **c.** whales

4. How many movies are showing at the Golden Lion Movie Studio?
   a. ten   **b.** four   **c.** three

3 LISTEN AND UNDERSTAND 🎧 CD 2 Track 19

A. A group of tourists are visiting Angkor Wat in Cambodia. Listen to the guide give information and check (✓) the topics he talks about.

1. climate in the area ___
2. age of the temple ___
3. language the people spoke ___
4. sports played at the temple ___
5. reason they abandoned the temple ___
6. restoration of the temple ___

B. Listen again. Circle the correct answers.

1. There are *around 50 / over 100* temples in the area.
2. The palaces and public buildings were made of *wood / stone*.
3. Angkor Wat was built in the *eleventh / twelfth* century.
4. *Hinduism / Buddhism* was honored at the temple.
5. The temple was abandoned in *1431 / 1432*.
6. The French started to restore the temple about *100 / 150* years ago.

4 TUNE IN 🎧 CD 2 Tracks 20 & 21

A. Listen and notice how people express uncertainty about facts.

> **A:** *Do you know when the main temple was built?*
> **B:** ***I think*** *it was in the twelfth century.*
>
> **A:** *How many temples are here?*
> **B:** ***I believe*** *there are more than a hundred.*
>
> **A:** *Do you know the religion of the temple?*
> **B:** ***It must be*** *Buddhist.*

B. Now listen to other conversations. Does the second person express certainty or uncertainty? Check (✓) the correct column.

	Certainty	Uncertainty
1.	☐	☐
2.	☐	☐
3.	☐	☐
4.	☐	☐
5.	☐	☐
6.	☐	☐

⑤ AFTER YOU LISTEN

A. What do you know about these places of interest? Answer the questions in the quiz.

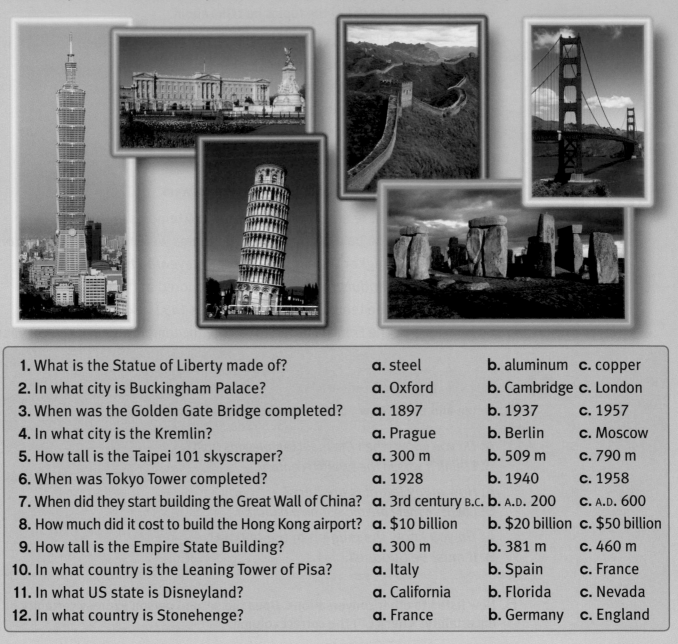

1. What is the Statue of Liberty made of?	**a.** steel	**b.** aluminum	**c.** copper
2. In what city is Buckingham Palace?	**a.** Oxford	**b.** Cambridge	**c.** London
3. When was the Golden Gate Bridge completed?	**a.** 1897	**b.** 1937	**c.** 1957
4. In what city is the Kremlin?	**a.** Prague	**b.** Berlin	**c.** Moscow
5. How tall is the Taipei 101 skyscraper?	**a.** 300 m	**b.** 509 m	**c.** 790 m
6. When was Tokyo Tower completed?	**a.** 1928	**b.** 1940	**c.** 1958
7. When did they start building the Great Wall of China?	**a.** 3rd century B.C.	**b.** A.D. 200	**c.** A.D. 600
8. How much did it cost to build the Hong Kong airport?	**a.** $10 billion	**b.** $20 billion	**c.** $50 billion
9. How tall is the Empire State Building?	**a.** 300 m	**b.** 381 m	**c.** 460 m
10. In what country is the Leaning Tower of Pisa?	**a.** Italy	**b.** Spain	**c.** France
11. In what US state is Disneyland?	**a.** California	**b.** Florida	**c.** Nevada
12. In what country is Stonehenge?	**a.** France	**b.** Germany	**c.** England

B. Work with a partner. Compare your answers. Use this conversation but include your own information.

A: *When do you think the Great Wall of China was built?*
B: *I think it was in the seventh century B.C. What is your guess?*
A: *I believe it was in A.D. 600.*

C. Check your answers below. Who in the class got the most correct?

ANSWERS: 1. c, 2. c, 3. b, 4. c, 5. b, 6. c, 7. a, 8. b, 9. b, 10. a, 11. a, 12. c

Lesson 2 Let's take a tour!

1 BEFORE YOU LISTEN

Circle the two places you would most like to see in New York City. Then compare with a partner.

1. **Times Square** The center of the city's entertainment and shopping district; nearly a million people visit every year to celebrate New Year's Eve.
2. **Guggenheim Museum** This unusual building opened in 1959 and exhibits modern art.
3. **Staten Island Ferry** This free ferry crosses New York Harbor every half hour during the week.
4. **Brooklyn Bridge** The first steel-wire suspension bridge in the world connects Manhattan and Brooklyn.
5. **Central Park** This park contains 26,000 trees and more than 275 bird species.

2 LISTEN AND UNDERSTAND 🎧 CD 2 Track 22

A. People are sightseeing in Hong Kong. Listen to the guide giving information about places on the tour and circle the correct statements. More than one answer is possible.

1. **Peak Tram**
   a. It was built in the nineteenth century.
   b. It is on the Kowloon side.
   c. It is a steep ride to the top.

2. **Star Ferry**
   a. It is not a very expensive trip.
   b. It crosses the harbor once an hour.
   c. You can go from Kowloon to Hong Kong Island.

3. **Ocean Park**
   a. It is the only amusement park in Hong Kong.
   b. You can enjoy different rides there.
   c. The guide does not recommend the Cultural Village.

4. **Stanley Market**
   a. It sells mostly goods from China.
   b. You cannot bargain there.
   c. There aren't any good restaurants there.

B. Listen again. Check (✓) the question that you think a visitor will most likely ask.

1. a. How often does it run? ____   b. How long is the show? ____
2. a. How much is the fare? ____   b. What is it used for? ____
3. a. What do they make here? ____   b. How long will we spend here? ____
4. a. How often do they come here? ____   b. What type of food do they have? ____

3 LISTEN AND UNDERSTAND 🎧 CD 2 Track 23

A. People are talking about places they visited. Did they enjoy their visit? Listen and check (✓) the correct column.

	Enjoyed	Didn't enjoy
1. the cultural center	☐	☐
2. the zoo	☐	☐
3. the science museum	☐	☐
4. the night market	☐	☐

B. Listen again. Are these statements true or false? Write *T* (true) or *F* (false).

1. a. Bob thinks the displays are fascinating. ___
   b. Bob did not stay at the cultural center all day. ___

2. a. All of the animals are in big open spaces. ___
   b. You can easily see everything in half a day. ___

3. a. There are interactive activities for children. ___
   b. Karen had just enough time to see the space rocket. ___

4. a. The market was very busy. ___
   b. The market does not sell any souvenirs. ___

4 TUNE IN 🎧 CD 2 Tracks 24 & 25

A. Listen and notice how people give positive and negative recommendations.

> ### What did you think of it?
>
> | Positive recommendation | Negative recommendation |
> |---|---|
> | *I'd recommend it to anyone.* | *I wouldn't recommend it.* |
> | *I'd suggest you try it.* | *I wouldn't suggest it to anyone.* |
> | *It's a good place to try.* | *It's not worth trying.* |

B. Now listen to other conversations. Does the person give a positive or a negative recommendation? Circle the correct answer.

1. a. Positive   **b.** Negative
2. a. Positive   **b.** Negative
3. a. Positive   **b.** Negative
4. a. Positive   **b.** Negative
5. a. Positive   **b.** Negative
6. a. Positive   **b.** Negative

A. Work with a partner. What recommendations would you give someone who is looking for these places in your town? Write your answers.

1. a good place to stay _____
2. a good place to eat _____
3. a place to buy handicrafts _____
4. a place to find some souvenirs _____
5. an interesting market _____
6. a nice area to go for a walk _____
7. a place to get some exercise _____
8. a place to get a view of the town _____

B. Role-play. You are in a tourist office. Take turns asking and answering questions about places to visit. Use this conversation but include your own information.

A: *Good morning. Can I help you?*

B: *Yes. I'm looking for a good place to stay. What would you suggest?*

A: *I'd recommend the Rex Hotel. It's very comfortable and it's in a convenient location.*

B: *OK. Thank you. I'm also looking for a good place to eat. Where can I go?*

A: *I suggest you try the Yellow Sun Cafe. It has really delicious food.*

B: *Great. And I would like to buy some handicrafts. Where should I go?*

A: *A good place to try is the local arts and crafts market downtown.*

B: *Where can I find some souvenirs?*

A: *. . .*

Transportation

LESSON OBJECTIVES
▸ Understanding opinions about places
▸ Understanding suggestions for improvements
▸ Giving suggestions

Lesson 1 How do you get to school?

1 BEFORE YOU LISTEN

A. Do you know these facts about transportation in the US? Check (✓) the two that you find the most surprising.

1. Ten million people use public transportation each working day. ___
2. If all the people who take public transportation drove their cars instead, their cars would make a traffic line 37,000 kilometers long. ___
3. The average driver spends about one hour a day in a car, including weekends. ___
4. People spend more than 100 hours commuting to work each year. ___
5. Fifty percent of 16-year-olds have a driver's license. ___
6. Sitting in traffic congestion costs travelers and businesses $40 billion every year. ___
7. There are more than 160,000 traffic signals in the country. ___
8. Forty percent of people in rural districts have no access to public transportation. ___

B. How much time do you spend each day traveling to and from work or school?

2 LISTEN AND UNDERSTAND 🎧 CD 2 Track 26

A. Students at a language school are talking about public transportation in their home cities. Listen and circle if they are satisfied with the forms of transportation.

1. **a.** trains **b.** buses **c.** taxis
2. **a.** subway **b.** buses **c.** taxis
3. **a.** subway **b.** taxis **c.** buses

B. Listen again. Check (✓) the correct answers. More than one answer is possible.

1. **a.** Train service is unreliable. ___
   b. The trains are clean. ___
   c. They need more trains. ___
   d. Taxi drivers drive too slow. ___
2. **a.** The subway system is very new. ___
   b. Trains are not air-conditioned. ___
   c. Buses are too old. ___
   d. It's difficult to get taxis on the street. ___
3. **a.** The subway is not very popular. ___
   b. Taxis are expensive. ___
   c. Trains are sometimes late. ___
   d. Buses are often delayed. ___

LISTEN AND UNDERSTAND 🎧 CD 2 Track 27

A. A radio announcer is reporting about London's solution to traffic congestion. Listen and write the correct numbers.

1. The congestion area is _____ kilometers.
2. There are _____ entrances and exits.
3. There are _____ cameras.
4. The toll is about _____ dollars before 10 P.M.
5. At midnight, the toll goes up to _____ dollars.

B. Listen again. Check (✓) the correct statement.

1. **a.** The results have been very good. ___
   b. The city is thinking of ending the project. ___

2. **a.** The photos go to a central computer. ___
   b. The photos are collected by the police. ___

3. **a.** The toll is paid at the police station. ___
   b. There are many ways to pay the toll. ___

4. **a.** The tolls become expensive very quickly. ___
   b. The tolls do not go up for a few days. ___

5. **a.** There will be a lot of money collected. ___
   b. A small amount of money collected will go to charity. ___

4 TUNE IN 🎧 CD 2 Tracks 28 & 29

A. Listen and notice how people give suggestions.

> *They really **ought to** get some new trains.*
> *They **need to** do something about the bus service.*
> *I think they **should** get newer buses.*
> *I think **it would be good if** they got new buses.*
> *They **shouldn't** use such old buses.*

B. Now listen to people giving suggestions. Circle the phrases you hear.

1. **a.** ought to   **b.** need to
2. **a.** should   **b.** it would be good if
3. **a.** should   **b.** need to
4. **a.** should   **b.** shouldn't
5. **a.** ought to   **b.** it would be good if
6. **a.** ought to   **b.** need to

A. What do you think of transportation in your area? Check (✓) the correct column. For transportation that you think is not very good, think of a suggestion for improving it.

	Pretty good	OK	Not very good
1. train or subway system	☐	☐	☐
2. buses	☐	☐	☐
3. roads	☐	☐	☐
4. taxis	☐	☐	☐
5. facilities for the disabled	☐	☐	☐
6. facilities for pedestrians	☐	☐	☐
7. sidewalks	☐	☐	☐
8. parking facilities	☐	☐	☐
9. facilities for bicycles	☐	☐	☐

B. Work with a partner. Take turns asking and answering questions about transportation in your area. Use this conversation but include your own information and ideas.

A: *What do you think of the subway system?*

B: *It's pretty good.*

A: *Really? I don't think it's very good. They should make the trains go faster.*

B: *That's a good idea. What do you think of the buses?*

A: *Well, they're not very good, either.*

B: *Yeah, I agree. It would be good if they bought some new buses.*

A: *How about the roads?*

B: *. . .*

LESSON OBJECTIVES
▸ Understanding information about places
▸ Following descriptions of experiences
▸ Changing the subject

Lesson 2 How did you get there?

1 BEFORE YOU LISTEN

What do you know about transportation around the world? Circle the statements that you think are false. Then check your answers below.

1. The longest direct commercial flight in the world is from New York to Singapore (about 18 hours).
2. Fast speed trains in Japan can reach a speed of over 300 kilometers per hour.
3. London has the oldest subway system in the world. It opened in 1863.
4. The tallest cruise ships are 15 stories high.
5. It takes one hour to cross from London to Paris using the Channel Tunnel.
6. It takes a week to travel across Russia by train.
7. Singapore International Airport has a swimming pool for passengers to use.
8. Many cities in England have triple-decker buses.

2 LISTEN AND UNDERSTAND 🎧 CD 2 Track 30

A. A guide is describing the Owls Head Transportation Museum in Maine, US. Circle the activities you think visitors can do at the museum. Then listen and check your answers.

1. see exhibitions
2. fly in old aircraft
3. buy unusual road signs
4. watch movies
5. attend lectures
6. attend workshops
7. ride animals
8. buy an antique car
9. borrow books
10. help repair old cars

B. Listen again. Are these statements true or false? Write *T* (true) or *F* (false).

1. There are no bicycles on display at the museum. ___
2. There are many modern items on display. ___
3. The workshops take about an hour. ___
4. Volunteers help rebuild old airplanes. ___
5. Cars can be purchased in the museum store. ___

ANSWERS: **5.** false, over two hours; **8.** false, only in *Harry Potter* movies

3 LISTEN AND UNDERSTAND 🎧 CD 2 Track 31

A. People are talking about different types of transportation they have experienced. Listen and number the types of transportation from 1 to 3. Two extra types of transportation in the list.

a. a cable car ride ___   **c.** a bus trip ___   **e.** a plane trip ___
b. a train trip ___   **d.** a ferry trip ___

B. Listen again. Circle the correct information.

1. **a.** At the beginning she was *terrified / amused / nervous*.
   b. The food they served was *fantastic / good / terrible*.
   c. Most of the time the trip was *smooth / bumpy / extremely uncomfortable*.

2. **a.** During the trip they saw *a lot / a little / nothing*.
   b. The other passengers were *rude / arrogant / friendly*.
   c. She found it difficult to sleep because the sea was *noisy / rough / short*.

3. **a.** The sleeping car was *tiny / uncomfortable / comfortable*.
   b. The food they served was *awful / OK / great*.
   c. The cars are *very new / a few years old / quite old*.

4 TUNE IN 🎧 CD 2 Tracks 32 & 33

A. Listen and notice how people change the subject.

> *At any rate, you survived your first trip.*
> *Anyway, I want to show you pictures of the islands.*
> *Anyhow, let's get started.*
> *In any case, you should check it out.*

B. Now listen to people change the subject. Write the phrases you hear.

1. _____, let me tell you more about the food.
2. _____, the trip was a great success.
3. _____, it's easy to get there by taxi.
4. _____, it's worth it once you get there.

A. How many different types of transportation have you taken? Check (✓) the ones you have done.

1. flown in a helicopter ___
2. taken a long bus ride ___
3. ridden a motorcycle ___
4. ridden an animal ___
5. ridden on a cable car ___
6. taken the subway ___
7. been on a cruise ___
8. flown in an airplane ___
9. ridden a bicycle ___
10. been on a ferry ___

B. Work with a partner. Take turns asking and answering questions about transportation. Use this conversation but include your own information. Who had the most exciting experience? Who had the scariest?

A: *Have you ever flown in a helicopter?*

B: *Yes, a couple of times. I flew in a helicopter once when I was in New York.*

A: *Were you nervous?*

B: *Not really. I loved it. Anyway, what about you? Have you ever flown in a helicopter?*

A: *Yes, I have. It was the scariest experience of my life.*

B: *Really? Why?*

A: *Well, we almost crashed. Anyhow, have you ever taken a long bus ride?*

B: *. . .*

Relationships

LESSON OBJECTIVES
▸ Making inferences from key words
▸ Understanding descriptions of people's qualities
▸ Giving opinions

Lesson 1 Let's be friends!

1 BEFORE YOU LISTEN

A. What qualities do you think make a good friendship? Check (✓) the correct column. Then compare your answers with a partner.

Good Friends . . .	Very important	Important	Not important
1. listen to each other.	☐	☐	☐
2. don't criticize each other.	☐	☐	☐
3. understand each other's moods.	☐	☐	☐
4. have the same sense of humor.	☐	☐	☐
5. help solve each other's problems.	☐	☐	☐
6. give each other compliments.	☐	☐	☐
7. have the same educational background.	☐	☐	☐
8. don't disagree with each other.	☐	☐	☐
9. can rely on each other.	☐	☐	☐
10. have the same interests and hobbies.	☐	☐	☐

B. Which of these qualities does your best friend have? _____

2 LISTEN AND UNDERSTAND 🎧 CD 2 Track 34

A. People are talking about their friends. What qualities do they comment on? Listen and check (✓) the correct columns.

	Career	Appearance	Family	Interests	Education
1.	☐	☐	☐	☐	☐
2.	☐	☐	☐	☐	☐
3.	☐	☐	☐	☐	☐
4.	☐	☐	☐	☐	☐

B. Listen again. Which word best describes each friend? Circle the correct word.

1. **a.** self-centered   **b.** thoughtful
2. **a.** outgoing   **b.** critical
3. **a.** serious   **b.** superficial
4. **a.** arrogant   **b.** well-read

3 LISTEN AND UNDERSTAND 🎧 CD 2 Track 35

A. Friends are describing how they first met. Listen and number the summaries of their stories from 1 to 3.

Suzie & Terry

Andrew & Kazu

John & Maggie

a. They met through a friend and got along right away. They found they shared a lot of interests. ___

b. They met by chance. At first they had the wrong idea about each other, but later they found they had a lot in common. ___

c. They were introduced by a friend. They don't like many of the same things, but they still get along very well. ___

B. Listen again. Which people do these statements describe? Check (✓) the correct column. More than one answer is possible.

	Andrew & Kazu	John & Maggie	Suzie & Terry
1. They both enjoy dancing.	☐	☐	☐
2. They met on vacation.	☐	☐	☐
3. They met while playing sports.	☐	☐	☐
4. They met at a friend's place.	☐	☐	☐
5. They like the same types of movies.	☐	☐	☐

4 TUNE IN 🎧 CD 2 Tracks 36 & 37

A. Listen and notice how people give opinions.

> *It seems like/as if* he's really special.
> *It seems to me that* she's perfect for you.
> *I think* he's very sensitive.
> *If you ask me,* it sounds like she has a great career ahead of her.
> *I don't think* it's very easy to get to know him.

B. Now listen to people giving opinions. Circle the phrases you hear.

1. **a.** I think   **b.** I don't think
2. **a.** If you ask me   **b.** It seems to me
3. **a.** I think   **b.** I don't think
4. **a.** It seems to me   **b.** It seems as if
5. **a.** I think   **b.** I don't think
6. **a.** It seems like   **b.** It seems as if

A. What type of friend are you? Read the survey and (circle) the answers that are true for you.

5. You and a friend both want to run for the same position in a school club. Do you…
a. ask your friend not to run?
b. compete with your friend?
c. let your friend run?

6. You and a friend both have romantic feelings toward the same person. Do you…
a. talk about it with your friend?
b. go on a date with the person you both like?
c. decide not to pursue your feelings?

1. You meet someone you would like to be friends with. Do you…
a. introduce yourself?
b. ask someone to introduce you?
c. hope they will introduce themselves?

2. A friend has a habit that annoys you. Do you…
a. talk to your friend about it?
b. talk to another friend about it?
c. ignore it?

7. A friend wants to spend too much time with you and you don't have time for your other friends. Do you…
a. discuss it with your friend?
b. stop seeing your friend?
c. ignore it?

3. A friend has been saying false things about you behind your back. Do you…
a. ask them to explain?
b. end the friendship?
c. ignore it?

8. A friend wants to copy your work for a class assignment. Do you…
a. offer to help the friend with the assignment?
b. not let the friend copy it?
c. let the friend copy it?

4. A friend invites you to see a movie, then cancels, and then you find out they went with someone else. Do you…
a. ask them about it?
b. do something to get back at them?
c. ignore it?

SCORES
Mostly As: You are an outgoing and open-minded friend. You are good at communicating and problem-solving.

Mostly Bs: You are a confident friend. You are sure of yourself and independent.

Mostly Cs: You are a supportive friend. You don't like to criticize and you are good at avoiding conflict.

B. Work with a partner. Decide which is the best answer to each question in the survey. Use this conversation but include your own information.

A: *What's the best thing to do if you meet someone you would like to be friends with?*
B: *If you ask me, the best thing to do is introduce yourself. What do you think?*
A: *I think you should ask someone to introduce you.*
B: *Yeah, you're probably right.*
A: *What's the best thing to do if your friend has a habit that annoys you?*
B: . . .

LESSON OBJECTIVES
▸ Understanding facts about weddings
▸ Following descriptions of weddings
▸ Expressing preferences

Lesson 2 How was the wedding?

1 BEFORE YOU LISTEN

What is important to you when you go to a wedding? Rank this list from 1 (most important) to 7 (least important). Then compare your answers with a partner.

___ There is plenty to eat and drink for the guests.
___ The ceremony is held in a church or temple.
___ The bride and groom are in traditional wedding clothes.
___ The location is nicely decorated and has plenty of flowers.
___ There is live music.
___ There are lots of guests and there is a big party after the ceremony.
___ The bride and groom write their own vows.

2 LISTEN AND UNDERSTAND CD 2 Track 38

A. Someone is describing a traditional American wedding. Number the events from 1 to 8 in the order you think they happen. Then listen and check your answers.

a. The guests throw rice at the couple. ___
b. The bride arrives at the church. ___
c. The bride throws her flower bouquet. ___
d. The bride and groom kiss. ___
e. The guests go to the church. ___
f. The guests go to the reception. ___
g. The bride's father escorts her to the front of the church. ___
h. The groom and the groomsmen wait at the church. ___

B. Listen again. Circle the correct answer.

1. What color dresses do bridesmaids wear?
　a. white　　　**b.** another color
2. Who sits on the left side of the church?
　a. friends of the bride　　**b.** friends of the groom
3. Who arrives with the groom?
　a. the bride　　**b.** the best man
4. When do the guests throw rice?
　a. as the couple arrives　　**b.** as the couple leaves
5. When do people give speeches?
　a. during the ceremony　　**b.** during the reception
6. Who tries to catch the bouquet?
　a. only the bridesmaids　　**b.** single women

3 LISTEN AND UNDERSTAND 🎧 CD 2 Track 39

A. People are talking about unusual weddings they attended. Listen and check (✓) the correct information for each wedding.

	1	2	3	4
a. The couple wore traditional wedding clothes.	☐	☐	☐	☐
b. There was music.	☐	☐	☐	☐
c. The ceremony was not inside.	☐	☐	☐	☐
d. They rode animals.	☐	☐	☐	☐
e. The couple wasn't standing on the ground.	☐	☐	☐	☐
f. There was a party after the ceremony.	☐	☐	☐	☐

B. Listen again. Are these statements true or false? Write *T* (true) or *F* (false).

1. The couple got married in the country where they first met. ___
2. The guests and the couple were underwater. ___
3. The wedding cost a lot of money. ___
4. The couple got married at the clubhouse. ___

4 TUNE IN 🎧 CD 2 Tracks 40 & 41

A. Listen and notice how people talk about preferences.

> A: *Would you prefer* a traditional wedding or a nontraditional wedding?
> B: *I'd prefer* a traditional wedding.
>
> A: *Would you rather* have a big wedding or a small one?
> B: *I'd rather have* a big wedding.

B. Now listen to people express preferences. Number the statements you hear from 1 to 6.

a. I think I'd prefer to have one overseas. ___
b. I'd rather marry someone who is a bit different from me. ___
c. I think I'd prefer a long one. ___
d. I'd prefer a small wedding. ___
e. I'd rather have traditional music at a wedding. ___
f. I'd prefer someone a little younger, I think. ___

A. What type of wedding would you prefer to have? Complete the survey for yourself.

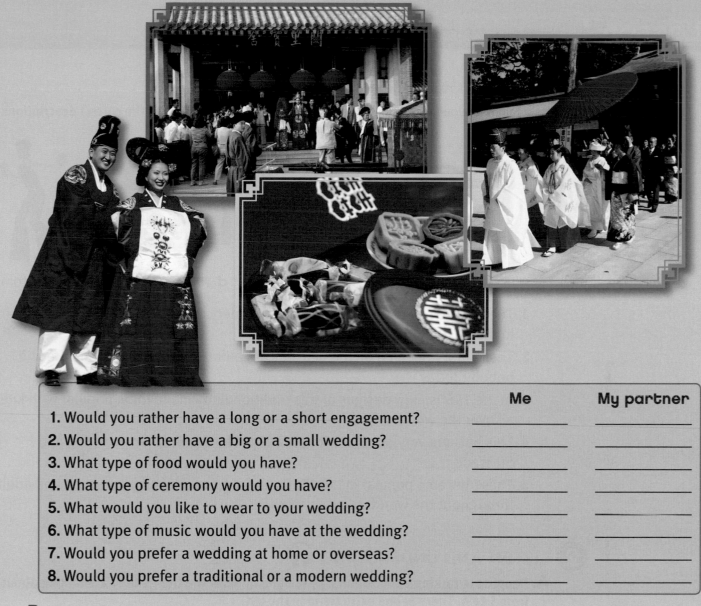

	Me	My partner
1. Would you rather have a long or a short engagement?	_____	_____
2. Would you rather have a big or a small wedding?	_____	_____
3. What type of food would you have?	_____	_____
4. What type of ceremony would you have?	_____	_____
5. What would you like to wear to your wedding?	_____	_____
6. What type of music would you have at the wedding?	_____	_____
7. Would you prefer a wedding at home or overseas?	_____	_____
8. Would you prefer a traditional or a modern wedding?	_____	_____

B. Work with a partner. Take turns asking and answering the questions and complete the survey for your partner. Use this conversation but include your own information. How many of your answers are the same?

A: *When do you want to get married? Would you rather have a long or a short engagement?*

B: *I'd rather have a short engagement. About three months.*

A: *Oh, that's quick! Would you rather have a big or a small wedding?*

B: *I'd prefer a small wedding. Maybe with only about 30 people.*

A: *What type of food would you have?*

B: *I'd have traditional Korean food. It would make my parents happy.*

A: *What type of ceremony would you have?*

B: *. . .*

LESSON OBJECTIVES
▸ Making inferences from key words
▸ Understanding information about computer games
▸ Showing interest

Lesson 1 Do you remember them?

1 BEFORE YOU LISTEN

How much do you know about these trends? Match the words with the correct descriptions.

a. video games **b.** yo-yos **c.** skateboards **d.** reality TV **e.** bell-bottoms

1. These were based on the style worn by American sailors and became popular in the 1970s. ___
2. These first appeared on the beaches of California in the 1960s and are still popular today. ___
3. In the 1960s, new designs of this traditional toy made them popular with kids all over the world. ___
4. This became very popular with programs like *Big Brother*, *Pop Idol*, and *Survivor*. ___
5. These became popular in the 1980s and are now played by children and adults throughout the world. ___

2 LISTEN AND UNDERSTAND 🎧 CD 3 Track 02

A. People are talking about trends. Listen and number the things they are talking about from 1 to 4. There is one extra trend in the list.

a. reality TV ___ **c.** in-line skates ___ **e.** Pac-man ___
b. trampolines ___ **d.** crossword puzzles ___

B. Listen again. Circle the correct information.

1. **a.** It was named after *its inventor / a folk hero*.
   b. It was invented by *a Japanese company / an American inventor*.
2. **a.** They were first developed *in England / in Holland*.
   b. They were most often used for *exercise / transportation*.
3. **a.** They have been popular for *20 years / nearly 100 years*.
   b. They are commonly seen *in newspapers / on clothing*.
4. **a.** They are *actors / strangers*.
   b. It is *a competition / an old invention*.

A. A radio interviewer is talking to a representative of the video game industry. Listen and check (✓) the topics they discuss.

1. places to buy video games ___
2. amount of time people spend playing games ___
3. amount of money people spend on games ___
4. the reason games are popular ___
5. the most popular video games ___
6. dangers of playing games ___
7. places to play games ___
8. the most successful manufacturers ___

B. Listen again. Are these statements true or false? Write *T* (true) or *F* (false).

1. People usually spend about 15 hours a week playing games. ___
2. The speaker thinks games are good for the brain. ___
3. Most console game players are male. ___
4. Most game players are under 18. ___
5. Adventure games are the most popular. ___
6. People who play games watch fewer movies. ___
7. Most game consoles are kept in bedrooms. ___
8. The future of the game industry is not looking good. ___

4 TUNE IN 🎧 CD 3 Tracks 04 & 05

A. Listen and notice how people show interest.

A: *They're not just for young people.*

B: *That's interesting.*
B: *I bet they're not.*
B: *I didn't know that.*
B: *That's cool.*
B: *You don't say!*

B. Now listen to people showing interest. Number the statements you hear from 1 to 5.

a. I bet he did. ___
b. Oh, I didn't know that. ___
c. That's cool. ___
d. That's interesting. ___
e. You don't say! ___

A. Add statements of interest to the conversation. Then practice the conversation with a partner.

I bet.	I didn't know that.	That's interesting.
That's cool.	You don't say!	

A: *Have you ever seen a tamagotchi?*

B: *Yes, I think so. It's a virtual pet, isn't it?*

A: *Yes, that's right. A Japanese housewife invented it.*

B: _____ *Why did she invent it?*

A: *Because she wanted her son to have a pet that was easy to care for.*

B: _____ *Doesn't every mother want that? When was this?*

A: *In 1996. When it was first sold, people stood in line for hours to buy one.*

B: _____ *And how does it work?*

A: *You have to feed it when it's hungry, play with it when it needs attention, and scold it when it's been bad. And if you don't, it will become unhappy, cranky, sick, or even die.*

B: _____ *And what does tamagotchi mean?*

A: *It means "lovable egg."*

B: _____

B. What popular trends do you like? Complete the survey for yourself.

	Me	My partner
1. What computer or video game is your favorite?	_____	_____
2. What is your least favorite computer or video game?	_____	_____
3. What new game do you play with your friends?	_____	_____
4. What new technology do you want to buy?	_____	_____
5. What fashion do you follow?	_____	_____
6. What new sport are you interested in?	_____	_____
7. What reality TV show do you like?	_____	_____
8. What toys do your friends collect?	_____	_____

C. Work with a partner. Take turns asking and answering the questions and complete the survey for your partner. How many of your answers are the same?

LESSON OBJECTIVES
▸ Understanding features of offices
▸ Understanding supporting information
▸ Asking for clarification

Lesson 2 Get ready for the future

1 BEFORE YOU LISTEN

Have you heard of these trends? Match them with the correct definitions.

1. the virtual office ____

    a. the entire world connected by electronic communication

2. school-free education ____

    b. the percentage of elderly people in a population is growing rapidly

3. a cashless society ____

    c. a working environment that has no fixed location

4. the global village ____

    d. purchases are made by credit card or electronic funds

5. an aging society ____

    e. distance learning through electronic means

2 LISTEN AND UNDERSTAND 🎧 CD 3 Track 06

A. College classmates are discussing the virtual office and an aging society. Circle the topics you think they will discuss. Then listen and check your answers.

1. The virtual office
    a. size
    b. salary
    c. advantages
    d. Web sites

2. An aging society
    a. causes
    b. impact
    c. shopping
    d. taxes

B. Listen again. Are these statements true or false? Write *T* (true) or *F* (false).

1.   **a.** Workers do not communicate with each other face-to-face. ____
    b. The virtual office is completely different from a real office. ____
    c. The virtual office will be cheaper to run. ____

2.   **a.** Health care demands will be lower. ____
    b. In many countries thirty percent of the population will be over 65. ____
    c. People will work until they are very old. ____

LISTEN AND UNDERSTAND 🎧 CD 3 Track 07

A. A radio panelist is talking about the global village. (Circle) the questions you think she will answer. Then listen and check your answers.

1. What is the definition of a global village?

2. Why do people live in villages?

3. What has caused the global village?

4. What role has politics played?

5. Why is TV popular in some countries?

6. What role has technology played?

7. How many people live in the global village?

B. Listen again. (Circle) the factors the panelist says have helped make the world like a global village.

1. political change	5. free travel
2. cost of living	6. satellites and computers
3. end of communism	7. the Internet
4. advertising	8. health problems

4 TUNE IN 🎧 CD 3 Tracks 08 & 09

A. Listen and notice how people ask for clarification.

> **A:** *The world is becoming like one big village.*
>
> **B:** *What do you mean by that?*
> **B:** *Could you explain that again?*
> **B:** *Could you go over that once more?*
> **B:** *Could you run that by me again?*

B. Now listen to other conversations. Does the second person ask for clarification in each conversation? Check (✓) the correct column.

	Yes	No
1.	☐	☐
2.	☐	☐
3.	☐	☐
4.	☐	☐
5.	☐	☐
6.	☐	☐

5 AFTER YOU LISTEN

A. Put these sentences in order to make two conversations. Then practice the conversations with a partner.

Conversation 1

___ *Oh, I get it now! So students in the same class won't ever meet each other.*

___ *What do you mean by that?*

___ *School-free education means that all schools and universities will exist online.*

___ *Well, students will study and learn using the Internet at home. They won't go to school.*

Conversation 2

___ *Could you run that by me again?*

___ *Oh, OK. So we'll be able to pay all our bills online, too!*

___ *Well, we'll always use credit cards instead of cash or checks.*

___ *A cashless society means all banking and shopping is done electronically.*

B. Work with a partner. What will happen in the future? Rank these statements from 1 (most likely to happen) to 8 (least likely to happen).

___ Most people will work until they are in their eighties.

___ Everyone will work at home.

___ All students will have virtual teachers and classmates.

___ No one will ever carry cash.

___ Many people will rarely leave their homes.

___ Everyone will have online friends all over the world.

___ Many people will never have face-to-face contact with their boss.

___ Taxes will increase by 60%.

C. Work with another pair. Take turns talking about the statements in part B. Are your answers the same?

LESSON OBJECTIVES
▸ Identifying features of a business
▸ Recognizing business advice
▸ Using double questions

Lesson 1 Let's start a business

1 BEFORE YOU LISTEN

Would you buy any of these small businesses? Rank them from 1 (most interesting) to 6 (least interesting). Then compare your answers with a partner.

___ **Graphic Design Studio**
Staff of three, with active business for hotels, restaurants, and offices.

___ **Hair and Beauty Salon**
Good location, busy, staff of four. Regular clients.

___ **Cafe**
Serving light meals. Clients mostly office workers and students.

___ **Bookstore**
With coffee bar, staff of eight. Lively place. Open late and weekends.

___ **Teen Boutique**
Popular store near train station, specializing in young fashions.

___ **Photo shop**
Cameras and photo supplies, including photo studio.

2 LISTEN AND UNDERSTAND 🎧 CD 3 Track 10

A. Young business owners are being interviewed on a TV show. What kind of businesses do they have? Listen and number the businesses from 1 to 5. One extra business is in the list.

a. child tutoring center ___
b. guest house ___
c. flower shop ___
d. health food store ___
e. dance studio ___
f. teen boutique ___

B. Listen again. Check (✓) the correct information.

1. **a.** Matt just bought the business last year. ___
   b. Most of Matt's clients are in their 30s. ___

2. **a.** Clients are taught individually. ___
   b. The business is busy all year. ___

3. **a.** Risa finds the business difficult to run. ___
   b. The business is expanding the range of products they sell. ___

4. **a.** Young-hee runs the business with her parents. ___
   b. The business is really big. ___

5. **a.** Sarah's clients are all older. ___
   b. The business matches Sarah's interests. ___

A. A business consultant is talking about starting a business at home. Circle the questions you think she will answer. Then listen and check your answers.

    1. How much will it cost to run it?

    2. Who was the founder of McDonalds?

    3. How can I reach my customers?

    4. Why do people in some businesses wear uniforms?

    5. How much profit can businesses expect to make?

    6. What type of business can be run from home?

B. Listen again. Are these statements true or false? Write *T* (true) or *F* (false).

    1. Not all businesses involve physical products. ___

    2. The telephone survey business is growing. ___

    3. There is only one kind of cost involved. ___

    4. The profit from health foods is not high. ___

    5. Advertising is the best way to reach people. ___

    6. It's always necessary to advertise in magazines. ___

4 TUNE IN 🎧 CD 3 Tracks 12 & 13

A. Listen and notice how people use double questions to clarify what they are asking.

Opening question	+	Focus question
Is it a new business?	+	*I mean, have you had the business for long?*
What type of clients do you have?	+	*Are they mostly kids?*
What subjects do they need help with?	+	*Is it all subjects?*

B. Now match each opening question with its focus question. Then listen and check your answers.

Opening question	Focus question
1. Is your bookstore busy? ___	**a.** Do you have the same menu every day?
2. Is a music store a good business to own? ___	**b.** Are all the items new or are some secondhand?
3. What kind of people come to your salon? ___	**c.** Are there a lot of customers there most of the time?
4. What type of food does your cafe serve? ___	**d.** I mean, do you get all types?
5. What do you sell in your boutique? ___	**e.** Do you make much profit on each item you sell?
6. What are some problems involved with a cafe? ___	**f.** Is getting good staff a problem?

5 AFTER YOU LISTEN

A. How do you start a business at home? Write focus questions for the opening questions.

Opening question	Focus question
1. How much new equipment do you need?	_____
2. What type of clients will you have?	_____
3. Where will you advertise?	_____

B. Work with a partner. Which of the businesses in the box would be popular in your area? Choose one to run and complete the business plan.

computer programming	home-catering	translation
pet-sitting	T-shirt printing	music lessons

Equipment needed	Type of clients	Places to advertise
_____	_____	_____
_____	_____	_____
_____	_____	_____
_____	_____	_____

C. Work with another pair. Take turns asking and answering questions about your new business. Use the questions in part A. Which business will be the most profitable?

A: *Which business did you choose to run?*

B: *We chose pet-sitting.*

A: *How much new equipment do you need? Will you have to spend a lot of money?*

B: *Not at all. We will use the client's equipment.*

A: *. . .*

LESSON OBJECTIVES

> Understanding a talk about a company
> Understanding reasons for success
> Checking understanding

Lesson 2 The keys to success

1 BEFORE YOU LISTEN

Do you know these famous business people? Match the names with the correct descriptions. Then check your answers below.

a. Charles B. Wang   **c.** Russell Simmons   **e.** Coco Chanel

b. Dr. John S. Pemberton   **d.** Henry Ford   **f.** Oprah Winfrey

1. Entrepreneur of rap and hip hop music (1957–) ___
2. French fashion designer (1883–1971) ___
3. Shanghai-born computer software business owner (1944–) ___
4. Car manufacturer (1863–1947) ___
5. Inventor of Coca-Cola (1831–1888) ___
6. Top American TV celebrity (1954–) ___

2 LISTEN AND UNDERSTAND 🎧 CD 3 Track 14

A. A radio host is talking to a guest about the history of Coca-Cola. Circle the topics you think they will discuss. Then listen and check your answers.

1. the need to drink lots of water
2. the contents of the drink
3. how to bottle soda
4. how the company operates today
5. the person who invented the drink
6. the reason for the name
7. the history of the company
8. the role of women in business

B. Listen again. Answer the questions with no more than two words.

1. How many ingredients were in the original drink?   _____
2. What was added to the original drink?   _____
3. What are two main ingredients of the drink today?   _____
4. Did the inventor of Coca-Cola make a lot of money?   _____
5. Who supplies the ingredients today?   _____

ANSWERS: 1. c, 2. e, 3. a, 4. d, 5. b, 6. f

3 **LISTEN AND UNDERSTAND** 🎧 CD 3 Track 15

A. Young business owners are talking to a high school club. Listen and check (✓) the factors that are important for the success of each business they describe.

	Staff	Location	Products	Advertising	Clients
1. health club	☐	☐	☐	☐	☐
2. restaurant	☐	☐	☐	☐	☐
3. cafe	☐	☐	☐	☐	☐
4. boutique	☐	☐	☐	☐	☐

B. Listen again. Which businesses do the statements describe? More than one answer is possible. The first one is done for you.

a. It provides food. ___ ___

1. health club   **b.** It has grown a lot recently. _1_ ___

2. restaurant   **c.** It is mainly for young people. ___ ___

3. cafe   **d.** It has been written about lately. _1_ ___

4. boutique   **e.** It is popular with business people. ___ ___

f. It offers more than one product. ___ ___

4 **TUNE IN** 🎧 CD 3 Tracks 16 & 17

A. Listen and notice how people check understanding.

A: *Our business is family-oriented.*	**B:** *So that means you have activities for people of all ages?* **B:** *So what you're saying is you encourage families to come together?*
A: *That's a secret that only a few people know, even today.*	**B:** *If I understand you correctly, you're saying it's still a secret?* **B:** *If I heard you correctly, very few people know the ingredients?*

B. Now listen to people checking understanding. Circle the phrases you hear.

1. a. If I understand you correctly   **b.** If I heard you correctly

2. a. If I understand you correctly   **b.** If I heard you correctly

3. a. So that means   **b.** So what you're saying is

4. a. So that means   **b.** So what you're saying is

5. a. So that means   **b.** If I heard you correctly

6. a. If I understand you correctly   **b.** So what you're saying is

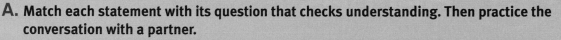

5 AFTER YOU LISTEN

A. Match each statement with its question that checks understanding. Then practice the conversation with a partner.

1. The staff make the business successful. ___

2. The business name is catchy. ___

3. The only thing that matters is the product. ___

4. The advertising is the key to success. ___

a. If I heard you correctly, nothing else is important?

b. So that means the people are important?

c. If I understand you correctly, you're saying the product isn't that important?

d. So what you're saying is it's easy to remember?

B. Work with a partner. What factors make a business successful? Think about the factors listed and add one of your own. Then rank the factors from 1 (most important) to 8 (least important).

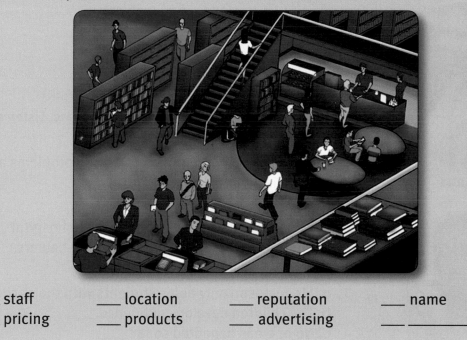

___ staff   ___ location   ___ reputation   ___ name

___ pricing   ___ products   ___ advertising   ___ _____

C. Name three successful businesses in your area. Decide with your partner what makes them successful. Use this conversation but include your own information.

1. _____   2. _____   3. _____

A: *I think Books, Books, Books is pretty successful.*

B: *I agree. One reason is its location.*

A: *Yeah, they are right near a university.*

B: *Another reason is their products. They only sell books that college kids like to read.*

A: *And I guess pricing is the other reason they are successful. They often have sales.*

B: *That's right. So what we're saying is it's the location, products, and pricing that make it so successful.*

LESSON OBJECTIVES
▸ Recognizing qualities of heroes
▸ Understanding the benefits of volunteering
▸ Responding to interesting information

Lesson 1 She's my hero

1 **BEFORE YOU LISTEN**

Which statements describe the qualities of a hero?
Check (✓) your answers and then compare with a partner.

1. They are inspiring and you look up to them. ___
2. They are educated. ___
3. They are generous and caring. ___
4. They are very young. ___
5. They are courageous. ___
6. They are concerned about others. ___
7. They are sincere and honest. ___
8. They are wealthy. ___

Anna

2 **LISTEN AND UNDERSTAND** 🎧 CD 3 Track 18

A. People are talking about their personal heroes. Listen and check (✓) the correct
statement.

1. **a.** Anna helps children who are having problems at home. ___
   b. Anna is paid for her work. ___
   c. Anna just started doing it. ___

2. **a.** Mrs. Yeh visits people who are in the hospital. ___
   b. Mrs. Yeh works with a group of other helpers. ___
   c. Mrs. Yeh is no longer doing it. ___

3. **a.** Mr. Simpson only helps students with their school subjects. ___
   b. The children develop confidence. ___
   c. No one has benefited so far. ___

Mrs. Yeh

B. Listen again. Who do you think does these things? Check (✓) the correct column.
More than one answer is possible.

	Anna	Mrs. Yeh	Mr. Simpson
1. gives up a lot of their free time	☐	☐	☐
2. helps people who are lonely	☐	☐	☐
3. helps children with problems	☐	☐	☐
4. probably needs a car	☐	☐	☐
5. works both with young and old people	☐	☐	☐

Mr. Simpson

3 LISTEN AND UNDERSTAND 🎧 CD 3 Track 19

A. A woman is talking about her experience as a volunteer. (Circle) the topics you think she will talk about. Then listen and check your answers.

1. how she started volunteer work
2. problems she had learning math
3. difficulties of doing volunteer work
4. need for special training
5. benefits of doing volunteer work
6. need for better science teaching in high school

B. Listen again. Check (✓) the correct column.

	Yes	No
1. Did she volunteer when she was a child?	☐	☐
2. Can she share her skills with others?	☐	☐
3. Has she learned new skills?	☐	☐
4. Has she learned more about life?	☐	☐
5. Does she have a lot of big problems?	☐	☐
6. Has she made new friends?	☐	☐

4 TUNE IN 🎧 CD 3 Tracks 20 & 21

A. Listen and notice how people respond to interesting information.

> **A:** She's very caring and she has helped a lot of people.
> **B:** *That's wonderful. How has she done that?*
>
> **A:** Mrs. Yeh is a real hero in the community.
> **B:** *Is that right? What has she done to help?*
>
> **A:** He was one of the most influential people in my life.
> **B:** *Really? What did he do to influence you?*

B. Now match each statement with its follow-up question. Then listen and check your answers.

1. I think nurses are heroes. ___

2. My dog saved my life a few years ago. ___

3. My brother is my hero. ___

4. My mother has inspired me the most in life. ___

5. My girlfriend rescued a child from a fire. ___

6. My first math teacher was a real hero to me. ___

a. That's wonderful. How has she inspired you?

b. What did he do to make you feel that way?

c. Really? Do you still remember her name?

d. Oh? Are you interested in becoming one?

e. Is that right? How did he do that?

f. Wow! Were you with her when it happened?

A. Complete each statement with the name of someone you admire.

1. _____ has really done a lot to help other people. _d_
2. _____ is someone I have learned a lot from in my life. ___
3. _____ is an athlete who is also a hero to me. ___
4. _____ is someone my own age who I most admire. ___
5. _____ is an entertainer who I think is also a hero. ___
6. _____ is one of the most inspiring leaders in the world today. ___

B. Match each statement in part A with its response. The first one is done for you. Then answer the follow-up questions.

a. I see. And what do you admire about him/her? _____

b. That's interesting. Why is he/she a hero to you? _____

c. Oh? How is he/she inspiring? _____

d. Really! How do you think he/she helped people? _____

e. That's wonderful. And why do you think he/she is also a hero? _____

f. Yeah? What have you learned from him/her? _____

C. Work with a partner. Take turns asking and answering questions about people you admire. Use this conversation but include your own information from parts A and B.

A: *Nelson Mandela has really done a lot to help other people.*

B: *Really? How do you think he has helped people?*

A: *He has helped people by working for peace and standing against racism in South Africa.*

B: *My father is someone I have learned a lot from in my life.*

A: *Yeah? What have you learned from him?*

B: *I've learned that you must always respect all kinds of people.*

A: *Yeong-ok is someone my own age who I most admire.*

B: *. . .*

LESSON OBJECTIVES
▸ Following details of a story
▸ Identifying facts about an organization
▸ Expressing appreciation

Lesson 2 Thanks for your help

1 BEFORE YOU LISTEN

Match the Website slogans with the correct descriptions.

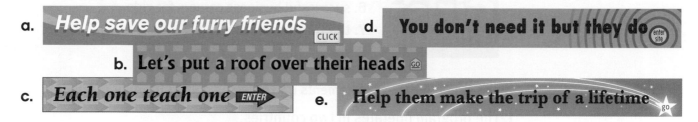

a. **Help save our furry friends** CLICK

b. **Let's put a roof over their heads** GO

c. **Each one teach one** ENTER▶

d. **You don't need it but they do** enter site

e. **Help them make the trip of a lifetime** go

1. Children with cancer go on a vacation paid for by funds raised by a health club. ___

2. Stray dogs are rescued by people donating their time on the weekend. ___

3. Earthquake victims receive food and clothing from money raised by people selling some of their possessions. ___

4. Prisoners are taught how to read by volunteer college students. ___

5. Homeless people stay in shelters paid for by children selling drinks on the street. ___

2 LISTEN AND UNDERSTAND 🎧 CD 3 Track 22

A. A TV reporter is interviewing a man who received some help from Habitat for Humanity. Listen and circle the correct answer.

1. How many children does Robert have?
   a. three daughters
   b. two daughters
   c. three sons

2. What happened to their house?
   a. It caught on fire.
   b. It was damaged in a storm.
   c. It was too small.

3. How did the organization help Robert?
   a. They gave Robert a new job.
   b. They gave Robert a lot of money.
   c. They rebuilt Robert's house.

B. Listen again and check (✓) *Yes, No,* or *Don't know* (if not enough information is given).

	Yes	No	Don't know
1. Are the children under seven years old?	☐	☐	☐
2. Was Robert's wife injured?	☐	☐	☐
3. Did Robert have insurance?	☐	☐	☐
4. Do the volunteers get paid?	☐	☐	☐
5. Was Robert grateful for the help?	☐	☐	☐
6. Did the family have to pay for anything?	☐	☐	☐

3 LISTEN AND UNDERSTAND 🎧 CD 3 Track 23

A. People are discussing an organization called Girls on the Run. Circle the topics you think the speaker will discuss. Then listen and check your answers.

1. the goals of the program
2. location
3. entering the movie industry
4. problems girls face growing up
5. the importance of positive thinking
6. successful business careers for girls
7. the purpose of running
8. dating tips

B. Listen again. Are these statements true or false? Write *T* (true) or *F* (false).

1. The program operates in two countries. ___
2. Each program runs for a couple of weeks. ___
3. Girls don't pay attention to the pictures they see in advertisements. ___
4. The program has activities in addition to running. ___
5. The program teaches girls to think positively about themselves. ___

4 TUNE IN 🎧 CD 3 Tracks 24 & 25

A. Listen and notice how people express appreciation.

	B: *That's really kind of you.*
	B: *That's very nice of you.*
A: *I'd like to volunteer.*	**B:** *I'm very grateful to you.*
	B: *We really appreciate your help.*
	B: *Thank you for your help.*

B. Now listen to two conversations. Number the expressions of appreciation you hear from 1 to 3.

Conversation 1
a. They'd really appreciate that. ___
b. We're grateful for your help. ___
c. That's very nice of you. ___

Conversation 2
a. That's kind of you to say so. ___
b. We really appreciate your help. ___
c. Thank you for offering to help. ___

A. Work with a partner. Think of two things you could do to help each organization. Use the suggestions in the box and add your own ideas. Then think of an organization in your area and two ways you could help them.

help in the kitchen	bring toys	sing songs
play games	donate food	read stories

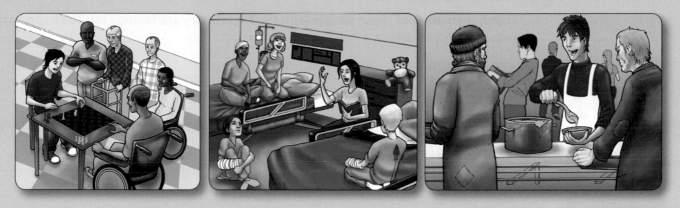

1. Metro Children's Hospital _____

_____

2. City Shelter for the Homeless _____

_____

3. Sunset Home for the Elderly _____

_____

4. _____ _____

_____

B. Role-play. You are calling the organizations in part A. Take turns offering help and expressing appreciation. Use this conversation but include your own information.

A: *Good morning. Metro Children's Hospital.*

B: *Hello. My name is Li-mei Ling. I'd like to volunteer.*

A: *Oh, that's really kind of you.*

B: *I'd like to read stories to the children.*

A: *That would be really good.*

B: *And also perhaps I could dress up as a clown and entertain the children.*

A: *That would be very useful, too. We really appreciate your help.*

LESSON OBJECTIVES
▸ Distinguishing given and not given information
▸ Understanding information about an explorer
▸ Expressing degrees of certainty

Lesson 1 What amazing people!

1 BEFORE YOU LISTEN

Match the names of these people with the events they are famous for. Then compare your answers with a partner.

a. Li-wei Yang   **c.** Tenzing Norgay   **e.** Jacques Cousteau

b. Jane Goodall   **d.** Amelia Earhart

1. This British-born woman went to Africa in the 1960s and spent the next 40 years studying the behavior of chimpanzees. ___
2. This famous pilot was the first woman to fly a plane solo across both the Atlantic and the Pacific Oceans. ___
3. This French explorer was famous for his discoveries of the world beneath the sea. ___
4. This astronaut flew into outer space in 2003. He completed 14 orbits of the earth and traveled more than 600,000 kilometers. ___
5. This Nepalese climber reached the top of Mount Everest in 1953. ___

2 LISTEN AND UNDERSTAND 🎧 CD 3 Track 26

A. Contestants are answering questions on a quiz show. Which contestant gives the correct answer? Listen and check (✓) the correct person.

	Mark	Emily	Kayla
Question 1	☐	☐	☐
Question 2	☐	☐	☐
Question 3	☐	☐	☐

B. Listen again. Check (✓) *Yes*, *No*, or *Don't know* (if not enough information is given).

	Yes	No	Don't know
1. **a.** Did he have hobbies when he was a child?	☐	☐	☐
b. Did he invent the Aqua-Lung by himself?	☐	☐	☐
c. Did he earn a lot of money from his invention?	☐	☐	☐
2. **a.** Was he born in France?	☐	☐	☐
b. Did he enjoy his stay in China?	☐	☐	☐
c. Did people believe everything he wrote?	☐	☐	☐
3. **a.** Did she go to college?	☐	☐	☐
b. Did she climb Mt. Everest by herself?	☐	☐	☐
c. Did she have any injuries while climbing?	☐	☐	☐

ANSWERS: 1. b, 2. d, 3. e, 4. a, 5. c

A. A teacher is talking about the life of the explorer He Zheng. Circle the topics you think the teacher will discuss. Then listen and check your answers.

1. when he lived

2. where he was born

3. where he traveled

4. who designed his parents' house

5. why he traveled

6. why museums are important

7. how many years he sailed

8. what he looked like

B. Listen again. Are these statements true or false? Write *T* (true) or *F* (false).

1. He Zheng was born in the fourteenth century. ___

2. He was born in a province near the sea. ___

3. He brought back gold and silver from foreign countries. ___

4. He sailed for about seven years. ___

5. He was reported to be very tall. ___

4 TUNE IN 🎧 CD 3 Tracks 28 & 29

A. Listen and notice how people express degrees of certainty when giving an opinion.

	Certain	Uncertain
He was an amazing explorer, wasn't he?	*Definitely.*	*Probably.*
	Of course.	*Maybe.*
	Sure.	*I'm not sure.*
	Absolutely.	*It depends.*

B. Now listen to other conversations. Is the second person certain or uncertain? Check (✓) the correct column.

	Certain	Uncertain
1.	☐	☐
2.	☐	☐
3.	☐	☐
4.	☐	☐
5.	☐	☐
6.	☐	☐

A. Why do you think some people risk their lives to explore the world or go on dangerous adventures? Check (✓) if you *Agree* or *Disagree* with the statements.

	Agree	Disagree
1. They are bored with everyday life.	☐	☐
2. They are curious about the world.	☐	☐
3. They just want to be famous.	☐	☐
4. They want to challenge themselves.	☐	☐
5. They are different from ordinary people.	☐	☐
6. They are trying to work through personal problems.	☐	☐
7. They are very confident and sure of themselves.	☐	☐
8. They have very strong religious beliefs.	☐	☐
9. They are looking for excitement.	☐	☐
10. They want to prove that they can do something different.	☐	☐
11. They like danger and like taking risks.	☐	☐
12. They are brave and not afraid of dying.	☐	☐

B. Work with a partner. Take turns asking each other about why some people take on dangerous adventures. Use this conversation but include your own information.

A: *Do you think they are bored with everyday life?*

B: *I'm not sure. What do you think?*

A: *Definitely. But I also think they are curious about the world.*

B: *Of course. I think so, too.*

A: *Do you think they just want to be famous?*

B: . . .

LESSON OBJECTIVES
▶ Understanding features of adventure tours
▶ Recognizing topics and main ideas
▶ Expressing preferences

Lesson 2 What an adventure!

1 BEFORE YOU LISTEN

Match each adventure trip with the phrase that best describes it. Then compare your answers with a partner.

a. the most unusual   **c.** the most exciting
b. the most challenging   **d.** the most comfortable

1.
JUNGLE SURVIVAL
Learn how to live in the jungle for ten days! Build your own accommodation and sleep in the trees. Your experienced guide will show you how to get your food from the jungle and out of the river. ___

3. **Mountain Climb**
Join guides to reach the top of the Olympic Mountains in the US in just five days! Enjoy the beautiful scenery as you trek up the mountain. Tents and food are provided. ___

2. *Castle Trail Ride*
Stay in a real castle at night and by day travel on horseback through the Irish countryside and forests filled with deer, pheasants, badgers, and foxes. You can even visit the most haunted castle in Ireland, if you dare! ___

4. *Mountain Bike Trails*
Cycle along the Wild Coast of South Africa and experience the wonder of nature firsthand. From your bike you can see a variety of different animals, including dolphins playing in the waves! ___

2 LISTEN AND UNDERSTAND   🎧 CD 3 Track 30

A. A travel agent is discussing different trips with customers. Listen and circle the correct information about each trip.

1. **a.** You sleep in hotels.   **b.** You do other things apart from hiking.
2. **a.** You use different forms of transportation.   **b.** It does not include snorkeling.
3. **a.** You stay in guesthouses.   **b.** You eat in high quality restaurants.

B. Listen again. On which trips can you do these things? Check (✓) the correct columns.

	Hiking trip	Island trip	Cycling trip
1. eat home-cooked food	☐	☐	☐
2. see mountain scenery	☐	☐	☐
3. stay with a local family	☐	☐	☐
4. stay away from home the longest	☐	☐	☐

3 LISTEN AND UNDERSTAND 🎧 CD 3 Track 31

A. Jun has just returned from South Africa and he is telling a friend about the trip. *Circle* the topics you think he will talk about. Then listen and check your answers.

1. the length of the trip
2. who he traveled with
3. things he saw
4. other trips he has taken
5. whether he enjoyed the trip
6. his study plans for next semester
7. the South African economy
8. whether he would recommend the trip to other people

B. Listen again. Are these statements true or false? Write *T* (true) or *F* (false).

1. Jun likes traveling by himself. ___
2. He was frightened during his trip. ___
3. He had a chance to drive a race car. ___
4. He rode in a safari car to look at the animals. ___
5. He enjoyed the cage diving. ___
6. He is planning to do the adventure trip in Hawaii next year. ___

4 TUNE IN 🎧 CD 3 Tracks 32 & 33

A. Listen and notice how people express preferences.

	States a preference	Doesn't state a preference
Would you prefer to stay with a local family or in a hotel?	**I'd prefer** to stay with a local family.	**It depends.**
Would you rather travel with a group or on your own?	**I'd rather** travel on my own.	**I'm not really sure.**

B. Now listen to other conversations. Does the second person state a preference? Check (✓) the correct column.

	Yes	No
1.	☐	☐
2.	☐	☐
3.	☐	☐
4.	☐	☐
5.	☐	☐
6.	☐	☐

A. How adventurous are you? Complete the survey for yourself. Number each statement from 0 (totally disagree) to 5 (totally agree). Add up your numbers and read your score. Then compare your answers with a partner.

LIVING ON THE EDGE

a. I love speed. ___

b. I like to take risks. ___

c. I like trying new things. ___

d. I would like to try bungee jumping. ___

e. I feel comfortable in unfamiliar situations. ___

f. I would be willing to touch a large snake or shark. ___

g. I don't mind uncomfortable accommodation and unusual food. ___

SCORES

0–10: Your idea of adventure is crossing the street.

11–20: You don't really like adventure, do you?

21–30: You have some potential as an adventure traveler.

31–35: You're a wild thing. Don't forget to get travel insurance.

B. Work with your partner. Take turns asking and answering these questions. Then choose one of the vacations for your partner.

City Break	Stay in a nice hotel with a pool in a nearby city
Beach Bliss	Stay in a high-class hotel on the beach
Mountain Trek	Stay in a guesthouse and go on a guided hike through mountains
Jungle Trails	Sleep in tents, eat food from the jungle, and go whitewater rafting

1. Would you rather travel to a hot climate or a cool climate?
2. Would you prefer to travel with friends or by yourself?
3. Would you rather stay in tents or a hotel?
4. Would you prefer to eat in restaurants or local markets?
5. Would you rather swim in a pool, sit on the beach, or go kite surfing?
6. Would you prefer to walk through a rain forest or go shopping?

Unit 15 Life Changes

LESSON OBJECTIVES
▸ Understanding descriptions of past events
▸ Identifying attitudes toward lifestyles
▸ Expressing degrees of uncertainty

Lesson 1 What was it like then?

1 BEFORE YOU LISTEN

Circle the two facts about life in the 1960s that surprise you the most. Then write two more aspects of life today that did not exist in the 1960s. Compare with a partner.

1. There were no Nike athletic shoes.
2. The Beatles were the most famous music group.
3. Men and women wore long hair.
4. There was no e-mail.
5. *The Sound of Music* was a top movie of the decade.
6. There were no home or laptop computers.
7. People got most of their news from radio and newspapers.
8. CDs and DVDs did not exist.
9. _____
10. _____

2 LISTEN AND UNDERSTAND 🎧 CD 3 Track 34

A. Teenagers are talking to their grandparents about life in the 1960s. Circle the topics you think they will talk about. Then listen and check your answers.

a. the cars they drove
b. the clothes they wore
c. the hairstyles they had
d. their high school teachers' names
e. the music they listened to
f. the textbooks they used in college
g. the social issues people thought about

B. Listen again. Check (✓) the correct information. More than one answer is possible.

1. a. The grandmother wore high heels and a miniskirt. ___
   b. The grandmother had short hair. ___
   c. The grandmother wore a brightly colored school uniform. ___

2. a. You cannot see this type of car in a museum. ___
   b. The grandfather kept the car for ten years. ___
   c. The grandfather got his first car at 18. ___

3. a. Coffee shops were popular meeting places. ___
   b. The word "hip" means "cool." ___
   c. The grandmother never went to a music festival. ___

LISTEN AND UNDERSTAND 🎧 CD 3 Track 35

A. A teacher is discussing social change with her students. Listen and (circle) the statements she would probably agree with.

1. Some things don't change as much as people think.
2. You should always do what your parents advise you to do.
3. Young people often want to show that they are different.
4. Young people dress much better nowadays than they did many years ago.
5. The way you look says something about your approach to society.

B. Listen again. Check (✓) **Yes**, **No**, or **Don't know** (if not enough information is given).

	Yes	No	Don't know
1. Did the teacher wear punk clothes when she was a student?	☐	☐	☐
2. Is Megumi wearing punk clothes today?	☐	☐	☐
3. Did the punk style begin in the 1970s?	☐	☐	☐
4. Is the punk style restricted to clothes, hair, and makeup?	☐	☐	☐
5. Does the teacher dress conservatively nowadays?	☐	☐	☐
6. Does the teacher still like the punk style?	☐	☐	☐
7. Does the teacher's father wear conservative clothes?	☐	☐	☐

4 **TUNE IN** 🎧 CD 3 Tracks 36 & 37

A. Listen and notice how people express degrees of uncertainty.

A: What year did they first come out?	**B:** *I suppose* it was in 1964.	*Less certain*
	B: *It could have been* around 1964.	↓
	B: *It was most likely* in the 1960s.	
	B: *I'm almost certain* it was in the 1960s.	
	B: *I'm sure* it was in 1964.	*More certain*

B. Now listen to people answering questions. Write the phrases you hear.

1. _____ it was sometime in the late 1990s.
2. _____ it was in 2002.
3. _____ the 80s.
4. _____ it's Joe.
5. _____ in the 1950s.
6. _____ it was in the early 90s.

A. What do you know about the twentieth century? Answer the questions in the quiz.

1. When did Madonna record her first hit song?	**a.** 1974	**b.** 1984	**c.** 1994
2. When was the movie *Star Wars* made?	**a.** 1977	**b.** 1987	**c.** 1997
3. What year did the first jumbo jet fly?	**a.** 1968	**b.** 1978	**c.** 1988
4. When were CDs invented?	**a.** 1963	**b.** 1983	**c.** 1993
5. When was the movie *Back to the Future* made?	**a.** 1965	**b.** 1985	**c.** 1995
6. When did the space shuttle *Challenger* explode?	**a.** 1966	**b.** 1976	**c.** 1986
7. When was the Internet created?	**a.** the 1970s	**b.** the 1980s	**c.** the 1990s
8. When was the cell phone invented?	**a.** 1973	**b.** 1983	**c.** 1993
9. When was the first MP3 player developed?	**a.** 1989	**b.** 1995	**c.** 2000
10. When did Hello Kitty toys become popular?	**a.** the 1970s	**b.** the 1980s	**c.** the 1990s

B. Work with a partner. Compare your answers. Use this conversation but include your own information.

A: *When did Madonna record her first hit song? In 1974, 1984, or 1994?*

B: *I suppose it was in 1974. What do you think?*

A: *I'm almost certain it was in 1984.*

C. Check your answers below. How many of your answers are correct?

ANSWERS: 1.b, 2.a, 3.a, 4.b, 5.b, 6.c, 7.a, 8.a, 9.a, 10.a,

LESSON OBJECTIVES
▸ Identifying important events
▸ Identifying changes in lifestyle
▸ Making assumptions

Lesson 2 How have you changed?

1 BEFORE YOU LISTEN

Have you done any of these things in recent years? Circle the ones you have done. Then compare with a partner.

1. changed schools
2. changed jobs
3. had a job interview
4. gotten a driver's license
5. moved to a new city
6. changed your hairstyle
7. started wearing glasses or contact lenses
8. gotten a credit card
9. left home to live on your own
10. achieved an educational goal

2 LISTEN AND UNDERSTAND 🎧 CD 3 Track 38

A. People are discussing important events in their lives. Listen and number the events from 1 to 4. There is one extra event in the list.

a. first semester in college ___

b. first date ___

c. first time in the hospital ___

d. first job interview ___

e. first day at work ___

B. Listen again. Check (✓) the correct statement.

1. a. Bill didn't plan at all. ___
   b. Bill was nervous. ___

2. a. Mi-young found it difficult at first. ___
   b. Mi-young was the only one who felt lost. ___

3. a. Jeremy met six people. ___
   b. Jeremy was on the wrong floor. ___

4. a. All of the people were jealous. ___
   b. Alice is related to the boss. ___

A. People are talking about an organization that gives loans so people can start their own businesses. (Circle) the topics you think they will discuss. Then listen and check your answers.

1. the name of the organization
2. how the program works
3. an example of a success story
4. some popular movie stars
5. difficulties faced by poor people
6. how a woman started a small business
7. how to prevent crime
8. how the business operates
9. what makes the business successful
10. shopping tips for visitors to Manila

Veronica

B. Listen again. Answer the questions.

1. How many children does Veronica have? _____
2. What was Veronica's income before her first loan? _____
3. What was the amount of Veronica's first loan? _____
4. What type of business did Veronica open? _____
5. What is one of the items Veronica sells? _____
6. How much was Veronica making after 18 months? _____

4 TUNE IN 🎧 CD 3 Tracks 40 & 41

A. Listen and notice how people make assumptions.

> A: *I found it pretty easy.*
> B: ***It sounds like*** *a good start.*
>
> A: *I really prepared myself.*
> B: ***You must have been*** *more than ready for it.*
>
> A: *So, yeah, it was difficult.*
> B: ***That's probably because*** *it was all new.*
>
> A: *I think I made a good impression.*
> B: ***I assume*** *it went well.*

B. Now listen to other people making assumptions. Number the assumptions you hear from 1 to 6.

a. I assume they bought you a car. ___
b. You must have gone out and spent it all. ___
c. That's probably because you were so nervous. ___
d. That must have meant a lot to you. ___
e. It sounds like you're ready to settle down. ___
f. I assume it got easier after the first day. ___

AFTER YOU LISTEN

A. What have you achieved so far? Write short answers to the questions.

1. When did you get your first cell phone? _____
2. What was your first part-time job? _____
3. When did you graduate from elementary school? _____
4. When did you first travel by airplane? _____
5. When did you go to a big city for the first time? _____
6. How old were you when you got your first bicycle? _____
7. How old were you when you got your first computer? _____
8. When did you meet your best friend? _____

B. Match the assumptions with your answers in part A.

a. I assume you were nervous about flying. ___

b. I assume you used it to play games. ___

c. It must have been exciting to get your first paycheck. ___

d. I assume your parents bought it for you. ___

e. I assume you have a lot in common. ___

f. You must have enjoyed seeing a different place. ___

g. You must have had a big party to celebrate. ___

h. I assume you found it difficult to ride. ___

C. Work with a partner. Take turns asking and answering the questions in part A and make assumptions. Use this conversation but include your own information.

A: *When did you get your first cell phone?*

B: *When I was 15.*

A: *I assume your parents bought it for you.*

B: *No, I bought it myself. I had a part-time job, so I saved some money.*

Student CD Track List

This CD contains the final **Listen and Understand** of each lesson.

Track	Unit	Content
01		Title and copyright
02	Unit 1	Lesson 1, *page 3*
03		Lesson 2, *page 6*
04	Unit 2	Lesson 1, *page 9*
05		Lesson 2, *page 12*
06	Unit 3	Lesson 1, *page 15*
07		Lesson 2, *page 18*
08	Unit 4	Lesson 1, *page 21*
09		Lesson 2, *page 24*
10	Unit 5	Lesson 1, *page 27*
11		Lesson 2, *page 30*
12	Unit 6	Lesson 1, *page 33*
13		Lesson 2, *page 36*
14	Unit 7	Lesson 1, *page 39*
15		Lesson 2, *page 42*
16	Unit 8	Lesson 1, *page 45*
17		Lesson 2, *page 48*
18	Unit 9	Lesson 1, *page 51*
19		Lesson 2, *page 54*
20	Unit 10	Lesson 1, *page 57*
21		Lesson 2, *page 60*
22	Unit 11	Lesson 1, *page 63*
23		Lesson 2, *page 66*
24	Unit 12	Lesson 1, *page 69*
25		Lesson 2, *page 72*
26	Unit 13	Lesson 1, *page 75*
27		Lesson 2, *page 78*
28	Unit 14	Lesson 1, *page 81*
29		Lesson 2, *page 84*
30	Unit 15	Lesson 1, *page 87*
31		Lesson 2, *page 90*